Am I Alone Here ?

NOTES ON LIVING TO READ
and READING TO LIVE

Peter Orner

Illustrations by Eric Orner

Catapult · New York

Grateful acknowledgment is made to the editors of the following
publications, where these essays first appeared in different form:
*The New York Times, The Atlantic, McSweeney's, Best of McSweeney's,
Buzzfeed, Guernica, Salon, The Millions, ZYZZYVA, Eleven Eleven, No
Tokens, The Rumpus* (as "The Lonely Voice"), and *Die Literarische
Welt* (Berlin).

Published by Catapult
catapult.co

ISBN: 978-1-936787-25-8

Catapult titles are distributed to the trade by
Publishers Group West, a division of the Perseus Book Group
Phone: 800-788-3123

Library of Congress Control Number: 2015955986

Printed in the United States of America

9 8 7 6 5 4 3 2 1

For Katie and Phoebe

and

In memory of my father

My education has been so unwitting I can't quite tell which of my thoughts come from me and which from my books, but that's how I've stayed attuned to myself and the world around me for the past thirty-five years. Because when I read, I don't really read; I pop a beautiful sentence in my mouth and suck it like a fruit drop, or I sip it like a liqueur until the thought dissolves in me like alcohol, infusing brain and heart and coursing on through the veins to the root of each blood vessel.

—Bohumil Hrabal,
Too Loud a Solitude

Contents

Am I Alone Here?

PENGUIN
BOOKS

FICTION

THE MAN OF PROPERTY

JOHN
GALSWORTHY

FICTION

COMPLETE

UNABRIDGED

Notes for an Introduction

Alone in the garage with all these books. There's no room on the shelves anymore. Now they live in piles. Technically, I'm a part-time resident of the apartment upstairs, but I spend many hours down here in what I call, without enough irony, my office. Our ex-neighbors used to film amateur porn in this space. When they moved away, they left behind powerful overhead lights (if I leave them on overnight, the place will burn down), and I sit here, awash in brightness, gazing at these stacks of books that will squash me when the big one comes, and I think: Earthquake or no earthquake, I'll be dead before I read a quarter of the books down here. I know this for certain and I wonder if repeating it out loud will make me believe it. *I'll be dead before I read even a quarter of the books down here.* That leaves at least three-quarters of these books unread. But to measure a life in unread books seems about right to me. All the experiences we will never have, places we will never go, people we will never meet. Even so, just to hedge my bets, I've asked my family to bury me with a decent library.

Down here, in addition to books, unused film supplies, boxes of condoms, unopened jars of coconut oil (intriguing), and velvet pillows, there are also snow tires for a car that no longer exists. There's a cracked bike helmet. Whose? Why hold on to a cracked helmet? And yet I don't toss it. I don't toss anything. I consider any and all objects fodder for some as yet untold story. Basically, I'm a hoarder with a highbrow rationale. This crap is for my art. There are suitcases (always good for a story), squash racquets, shovels, a single Rollerblade (size 13), a stained mattress, a cradle, and eight or nine cans of yellow paint. I'd once planned to repaint the kitchen. There's a large iron bell too heavy to move. Also, a saddle. Why a saddle? How long has this saddle been down here? Through how many decades of tenants? *An English saddle,* I can hear my father say. *See? There's an elegance to a saddle like this. It's got no horn, see? Horns are for slobs.* Here and there the gnawing mice peep out of their little holes in the walls. They're not afraid anymore. The cat that used to sleep on the couch died a month ago. I found her lying in her spot. She would always flee when I yanked up the garage door, leaving her indentation in the cushion for me to smooth my hand over. That's how I knew. When she didn't move when I opened the door. She'd been so thin for so long. I buried her—I never knew her name—in a patch of dirt behind our building. Now the mice come out and say hello. I say hello back. I say, Hey, I'm reading a great book by So-and-so. They shrug and retreat to their wood chips and rusty dust.

I've always been suspicious of introductions, prefaces, prologues, forewords, etc., as so often they seem a last-ditch effort to influence the way a book is read. Here's why the following book is worthy of your attention. The writer in question, in particular, is the last person in position to judge. It's like being your own lawyer. It only makes you look guiltier. And since I usually skip these myself, I wouldn't blame you for doing so, too, since I am now about to attempt what I've condemned others for trying to pull. Am I any less a hypocrite for confessing? But here's an attempt at self-explanation: In the year or so after my father died, I found, for the first time in as long as I could remember, I couldn't write fiction. My father and I were never especially close, and not nearly as close as he'd wanted us to be. For years he used to call me. Three, four, five times a day, he'd call and he'd call. I'd never pick up. But somehow this not being close, at least as far as I was concerned, *was* a form of being close. It helped define my precarious existence. There was always this gap between us. Within the gap: a kind of love. Now there's no gap, nothing. It never occurred to me that there wouldn't be a time when he wouldn't be puttering around the house I grew up in, winding the grandfather clock in the front hall or flossing his teeth in his blue bathroom. His sudden nonexistence left me with a blank I had no idea how to fill. Since it is my job to obliterate blankness with words, I felt adrift. My inability to do my day job—and fiction writing is my day-in, day-out job no matter how little it so often pays—may have had to do with the fact that in many ways my father had always been a fictional character in my life. Without him I lost my weirdest creation. My father's funeral in Skokie, Illinois, wasn't fictional. And I didn't invent the rabbi who'd never met the man he was eulogizing. It was early April and snowing. Light flecks of snow melted on my face like false tears. We dropped an urn filled with soot into a small, square hole and walked back to our cars.

Grief weighs heavy, regret even more, and I found that without a certain lightness I couldn't imagine my way into other people's lives. It was during those befuddled months that something occurred to me. Don't laugh. All these years of reading and trying to write, hours beyond hours of reading and trying to write, and one afternoon in a garage it hits me: the whole time I've actually been alive. How long did I think this dress rehearsal was going to last?

Somewhere along the line, these notes began to morph into something different from what I'd originally intended. I began them in 2008, at another time of great confusion, in the aftermath of a marriage, but they were never intended to be personal. They were only morning notes to myself. Think of this as a book of unlearned meditations that stumbles into memoir. After a while, this began (to appear) to have a certain logic. Only through reading has the rest of the world, including my own small place in it, begun to make any sense whatsoever. Stories say what I can't. A few years ago I came across the word "ekphrasis." It took me a couple of dictionaries to track down what it means, which is essentially art that attempts to describe other art. At first the word seemed pretentious, and I'm still unsure how to pronounce it, but I've come to see that maybe this is what I've been trying to do here, make some (poorer) art of other (greater) art as a means of explaining a few things to myself. Stories, both my own and those I've taken to heart, make up whoever it is that I've become. I'm a Jewish kid from Chicago, but without Anton Chekhov, without Isaac Babel, without Eudora Welty, without Juan Rulfo, without John Edgar Wideman, without Gina Berriault, without Malamud, Gallant, and Dubus (the list goes on and on and on*), I'm not sure I'd have any clue at all who I am. Yet even with them, some days, who the hell knows? There you have it. We've come full circle. I'm as confused as I was when I started. See what I mean about introductions?

One thing I'm sure of, though, is that I'm drawn to certain stories because of their defiant refusal to do what I just tried to do, that is, to explain themselves. Fiction isn't machinery, it's alchemy. Anybody who claims to shed complete light on the

---

*Hawthorne, Dickinson, Whitman, Jean Toomer, Sherwood Anderson, Akutagawa, Henry Green, Elizabeth Bowen, V. S. Pritchett, Devorah Baron, Camara Laye, Bruno Schulz, Felisberto Hernández, Joseph Roth, Elio Vittorini, Cesare Pavese, Natalia Ginzburg, Primo Levi, Italo Calvino, Bessie Head, Herman Charles Bosman, Dambudzo Marechera, Clarice Lispector, Ralph Ellison, Nelson Algren, Jane Bowles, J. B. Edwards, Elizabeth Bishop, Peter Taylor, Ida Fink, Alistair MacLeod, Penelope Fitzgerald, Henry Dumas, Marie Vieux-Chauvet, Danilo Kiš, Richard Yates, Grace Paley, Benedict Kiely, Guillermo Rosales, Larry Levis, Leonard Michaels, Zbigniew Herbert, Gwendolyn Brooks, Joseph Brodsky, Caleb Casey, Raymond Carver, Ryszard Kapuściński, Tillie Olsen, Evan S. Connell (who once wrote, "Stories speak with a thousand voices") . . . I sit surrounded, every day, by all these names on spines, names that alone are a kind of music, and so many left out, including all the living, and the as yet unread.

mechanisms by which fiction operates is peddling snake oil. A piece of fiction can have all the so-called essential elements, setting, character, plot, tension, conflict, and still be so dead on the page that no amount of resuscitation would ever do any good. Call this an anti-manifesto. Fiction doesn't work. There is no algorithm. No robot or supercomputer will ever write a moving story. Try and prove me wrong, Silicon Valley. Drive our cars, you'll never make us weep, because it is as impossible to explain precisely how a made-up story works or doesn't work as it is to explain love and not-love. Let's say you see a face in a crowd moving toward you. This particular face reminds you of someone out of your past, someone you once loved. Explain in words that moment of recognition? Or harder, infinitely harder, that moment of unrecognition? When this face gets closer and you realize the stranger isn't who you thought it was? When the vision in your eyes goes from lucid to foggy. Because the person you thought it was—she or he, whoever they once were to you—is gone. Long gone. Explain the moment when you apologize with your eyes because you don't have the strength to say it out loud? *I'm sorry, I thought you were—*

The other day at the park my daughter said to me, "You only love books and apples." I protested, saying that there are plenty of things I love as much as books and apples, dearly love, including, of course, her and her mother. I said being her father was by far the best thing that's ever happened to me once I got over the shock.

"What shock?"

"You know how much you love surprises. It's like that. You like them, you're just not always exactly prepared when they—"

"I'm always prepared."

"Look, bottom line is you got here, and you basically saved my life. All right? I just didn't—"

"Saved your life from what?"

"That's a longer story."

"How long?"

"The park will close before I even get halfway."

"Shorten it."

"Don't you want to go do the dizzy thing again?"

"Talk. Speak words."

"Let's just say I was on the edge."

"Of the pool?"

"In a way."

"Which pool? Woodacre?"

"A hypothetical pool."

"Where's that?"

"Montana."

"But you can swim."

"Sometimes people forget."

"What happens then?"

"Well, you kind of go to sleep in the water."

"You mean drown. Even when you can swim? Kaput?"

"That's it. Even when you can swim. Anyway, listen, you're better than any book. Got it? No joke. When we get home you can kaput all my books in the street."

She squinted her big eyes at me with a lack of faith that had no place in the eyes of a five-year-old. Maybe I wasn't all that convincing. I'd had to look up from a page to respond and, the whole time, held my place with my finger.

My dad also read. There were always piles of Dick Francis horse-racing mysteries beside his bed, but also novels by John Galsworthy. Horse racing I understood. My father had grown up riding and loved reading about the horses even more than the racing. He once said in another life he would have liked to have been a Canadian Mountie. But what drew him to Galsworthy and stories of intrigue and hypocrisy among the British upper crust? My father, from Fargo Avenue, Rogers Park, Chicago? How simple and irretrievable are the questions we never ask. What would it have taken for me to pick up the phone when he was still on the face of the earth?

JUNE 2015

I

SOMETIMES
I BELIEVE WE ARE
BEING TESTED

Hadn't my own experience taught me that no word can say as much as silence?

—Yasunari Kawabata, "Silence"

ANTON CHEKHOV

SELECTED STORIES

A SIGNET CLASSIC

CHEKHOV'S WAY OF DYING

I'm in the cafeteria of San Francisco General Hospital. I come here once in a while. It's a nice place to be distracted. I've been thinking about Chekhov, or trying to. I keep getting distracted. I have also come here today because I'm following up on a notion that in a hospital I'm closer to death than when I sit distracted in other places. I've seen no death today in this cafeteria. I've seen salads. Pudding. One of the doctors across the table from me is eating a bowl of strawberries while she tells another doctor about a third doctor's relationship with, it seems, a fourth doctor. Married, kids.

"She's so hard to talk to sometimes because her logic is so flawed. The crap she puts up with boggles the mind."

"Where's he based, this promiscuous pediatrician?"

"Parnassus."

"Apollo on his mountain. Should have guessed. Prick. Comes down and slums it at General."

Some patients down at the other end of the table keep high-fiving each other. I can't make out what they're celebrating. There—they did it again. High-five! There's also a man doing laps around the cafeteria, shouting into a cell phone. I've seen him here before. "I'm telling you," he shouts, "it's the military industrial prison complex. Eisenhower warned us of this in his final State of the Union. Ike, who would have thought he'd be the one . . ."

Chekhov is sometimes called with, to my ear, a tinge of dismissal a "realistic" writer. As if Chekhov was merely the sort of writer, a realistic sort of writer, who merely records what he sees. He does it pretty well—if you like that sort of thing. Realism (or realisticism?) is what is, plain and simple. I wonder if this idea doesn't give short shrift to experience itself by suggesting that there is some kind of objective reality that is the same for everybody.

And I don't just mean the guy talking about President Eisenhower. Another lap. Here he comes again. No, wait. Now he's talking *to* Eisenhower. *No, sir, they didn't heed you, sir. Not Lockheed Martin, not McDonnell Douglas, not Congress, nobody; they took your prophecy and stuffed it down the throats of we the people, plunked down another $3.5 million for a fighter jet—how many meatballs is that? Johnson said guns and butter, but he lied, while you, sir, you had the courage to call a spade a spade and nobody ever gave you a speck of credit because of course you helped create the mess in the first place, but at least you spelled it . . . No, sir, please, no false modesty, it was you . . .*

His reality (though pretty lucid, seems to me) is clearly different, somewhere far away, and though I would love to hear the grandfatherly voice he's communing with on the other end of that long-dead cell phone, what I'm trying to say is that your way of experiencing the world is subtly and vastly different from mine or the strawberry eating doctor's or the high-fivers', and that these alternate realities—the world seen through the muck of billions of different brains—encompass much of the wonder and freakishness of being alive.

Chekhov is as realistic a writer as Kafka, and vice versa. I read "The Metamorphosis" not as an allegory but as a rough morning. Gregor Samsa, you might want to call in sick today. Yet Chekhov, in his unobtrusive way, is often gloriously weirder. It's all in the things he notices about human beings, and there is nothing Chekhov does not notice. Few writers in history have been as gifted a noticer.

In 1890, Chekhov traveled to Siberia to examine and document conditions in the vast prison archipelago. It was a trip that biographers argue was terrible for his shaky health. The thirty-year-old Chekhov was already suffering from tuberculosis. Most likely nobody knew this better than Chekhov the doctor, but Chekhov the writer, Chekhov the citizen, was determined to observe firsthand the largest prison ever created. He'd go to Siberia if it killed him. The book-length investigation that resulted, *Sakhalin Island*, disappointed contemporary critics because it wasn't "Chekhovian" enough. But here, too, the man's eye is peerless.

> Traveling with me on the anchor steamer to Sakhalin was a convict in leg irons who murdered his wife. His daughter, a motherless little girl, aged six, was with him. I watched him when he came down from the upper deck to the WC, the little girl and the soldier with his rifle waited outside the door. When the convict climbed back up again, the girl clambered up behind him, hanging on to his fetters.

Chekhov is on a stated mission. Still, what rivets his attention is this tiny drama—tiny, but monumental—a little girl waiting outside the bathroom door for her father, a man who killed her mother. Chekhov makes no judgment about this moment, and we never meet these two again, and yet here they are, for all time, a prisoner and his little daughter.

The range and depth of this allegedly realistic writer is so vast, and so unprecedented, that if you feel as though by reading a bit of Chekhov you get the idea, you are missing out on a universe. It's like reading the first few lines of Genesis and thinking, Yeah, yeah, Eve eats an apple and all hell breaks loose for mankind, I think I got it. I'm no maverick. Who doesn't love Chekhov? Woody Allen once said:

> I'm crazy about Chekhov. I never knew anybody that wasn't! People may not like Tolstoy. There are some people I know that don't like Dostoevsky, don't like Proust or Kafka or Joyce or T. S. Eliot. But I've never met anybody that didn't adore Chekhov.

But isn't there something inherently suspect about being *the* writer everybody professes to admire? My theory is this: Easy to love from afar. Chekhov would be considerably less beloved if he wasn't so underread. You can't read "Lady with the Pet Dog" and call it a day. I'm thinking about the stories, the hundreds of lesser-known stories—not the five plays—and specifically of his incomparable late stories, when his work became considerably denser, often more sober, never without humor, yet wider in scope. It was as though, in his few remaining years, style itself became less and less important to him. These last stories seem, at first, almost to plod forward, until you realize—I'm not sure how to describe this exactly—that the pacing of the story has begun to match the cadence of your own breathing.

In 1902, the year Chekhov finished his second-to-last story, "The Bishop," He wrote to his wife, the actress Olga Knipper:

There's a frenzied wind blowing. I can't work. The weather has worn me out. I'm ready to lie down and bite my pillow.

He was forty-one. He had three years left.

As in many stories I can't live without, on the surface at least, not all that much happens. An important man—a bishop—reunites with his old mother, whom he hasn't seen in many years. Soon, as the reader knows from practically the first sentence, the bishop will die, and when he does, he passes without commotion in the course of an ordinary day. We'll all go the same way. You and me and the strawberry-eating doctor and the guy on the dead cell phone will die on a day when other people who haven't died will spend the morning answering a few e-mails before brushing the hair out of their eyes and thinking, Damn, it's already time for a haircut? I just had one the other—

So no, nothing earth-shattering occurs in "The Bishop," except that another human being leaves the scene of his life.

Dying, as opposed to death, you don't need me to tell you, is an isolating experience. It will separate us from those we love and those who love us. Nothing like a hospital visit to a dying parent to illustrate the demarcation line from those on the way out and those still here.

And when I think of my own death, I think of the people I'll leave behind, but I also mourn the impending loss of my routines. What struck me most today when I reread "The Bishop" was all the inconsequential things I won't do after I am gone. I won't wander the Mission District and rant stupidly, in my own head, about gentrification. *The horrors never cease. The techies reap destruction. What? Roosevelt Tamale Parlor is gone? It's over. San Francisco is over.* I won't sleepwalk into the kitchen for a Granny Smith in the middle of the night, and then eat it in bed, listening to the loudness of my own crunchings. I won't scratch the dog's pink belly and watch her go, erotically, apeshit. And this is the most tender and sorrowful aspect of "The Bishop." I would like to say terrifying also, but the bishop's dying days aren't scary, nor are they especially calm. They're plain normal. On Holy Thursday he officiates at church. He reads the gospels. He participates in the washing of the feet. He visits the widow of a general. He is driven in a carriage back home to the monastery. He drinks tea. He answers mail. He resolves a couple of petty disputes. He looks over some other documents. *What documents they were!* They came to him by the hundreds, thousands. He takes to his bed. He dies.

> Next day was Easter Sunday. There were forty-two churches and six monasteries in the town; the sonorous, joyful clang of the bells hung over the town from morning till night unceasingly, setting the spring air aquiver; the birds were singing, the sun was shining brightly. The big market square was noisy, swings were going, barrel organs were playing, accordions were squeaking, drunken voices were shouting.

But let's back up a little and linger longer with the man while he's still with us. And let's not be so deferential, either. If there is tension in this story, it's the fact that everyone, including his old mother (whom he has not seen in eight years), kisses the bishop's ass. Nobody will just talk to him like a regular guy. He wants a mother, not another fawning congregant.

His mood suddenly changed. He looked at his mother and could not understand how she had come by that respectfulness, that timid expression on her face: what was it for?

The only people who treat him like an ordinary person are old Father Sisoi, a man the bishop appreciates but at the same time dismisses as tedious and nonsensical, and his young niece, Katya. It's Katya who finally levels with him about why his mother has shown up out of the blue like this after all this time. The family back home needs his support. She's come for cash.

"Your holiness," she said in a shrill voice, by now weeping bitterly, "Uncle, Mother and all of us are left very wretched . . . Give us a little money . . . do be kind . . . Uncle darling . . ."

The kid's candor deeply moves the bishop and he agrees to help. After Easter, he says, we'll talk about it, child. The present action of the story revolves around the last mortal days of the bishop. But what makes this story so vivid, so alive, so celebratory, aren't the things the bishop does but the things he remembers.

I'll give a single minor, yet remarkable example, and then I'm leaving. I've had enough of hospitals for today. While lying in bed, the bishop has begun to retreat to the safety of his childhood back home in the village. But not in a way that you might imagine. Chekhov knows how this actually works, that what we remember is often as much an invention as any story we make up out of whole cloth.

He remembered the priest of Lesopolye, Father Simeon— mild, gentle, kindly; he was a lean little man, while his son, a divinity student, was a huge fellow and talked in a roaring bass

9

voice. The priest's son had flown into a rage with the cook and abused her. "Ah, you Jehud's ass!" and Father Simeon, overhearing it, said not a word, and was only ashamed because he could not remember where such an ass was mentioned in the Bible . . .

Hold it, that's not so strange. On first glance, maybe not. Would you take another look, though? This is a dying man, remember, and he's recalling an old priest from back home in his village and his oafish pig of a son, a divinity student who once— eons ago now—yelled at the cook. This is not epic deathbed stuff. These are peripheral characters that the bishop encountered early in his long and consequential life. These are the people who steal his attention in his last hours? And how does the bishop know that the upshot of that incident was not that Father Simeon defended the cook from his son but the comedy of the priest kicking himself for not remembering where in the Bible Jehud's ass appeared? Maybe Father Simeon once told the bishop this? I doubt it. Besides, the story marches on. Father Simeon is never mentioned again. A forgotten priest's brief shame over a detail he doesn't remember from the Bible is simply a part of another man's parade of memories. Two sentences and Father Simeon is retired from literature forever. I've spent more time on him than Chekhov does. I pause at the moment because I believe the bishop invented the detail, beautifully, out of whole cloth. Like his creator, the bishop himself is a fiction writer to the end. Even his own final memories have more to do with other people than himself.

Imagine yourself in the hospital. Maybe it's this crowded, noisy, fascinating mayhem of a city hospital. You've got plastic oxygen tubes stuck in your nose. You're wearing a catheter. Your family, at least those members of it that are still speaking to you, have solemnly gathered. With the drugs they've got you on, you hardly have the strength to open your eyes. Imagine you reach back, way back, and think about someone you hardly knew, an old neighbor—say, Mr. Chevy Millard, who lived down the block, a man you haven't thought about since 1977. Now say you dive into this Mr. Millard's head and give voice to one of his passing thoughts. Something like: "The sad truth is, if I hadn't inherited so much money, I might have followed my dream of becoming of a pianist like my idol Oscar Peterson."

See what I mean? Isn't this a bizarre thing to think about when you yourself are leaving the scene for good? But this is what happens in this story about a dying man—written by a dying man.

Tolstoy, who (generally) adored Chekhov,* once inferred that he might have been an even better writer if he had not been so dedicated a doctor. With all respect, Count, that's bullshit. Chekhov's being a doctor may well have been the key to how well he understood the connection between our ailing bodies and our ailing minds. To concern yourself with the hidden lives of others, including the long dead, especially at a time when you are trying to endure your own pain—is there a more generous act in life, in literature?

The night my grandmother died in a hospital in Chicago, she kept asking for someone named Jed. For hours it was: *Jed, Jed, Jed.* My mother finally figured out that Jed was a childhood neighbor in Taunton, Massachusetts, who died of hemophilia in 1918. It comes down to this. When we die, not only will our bodies be gone, but so will the people we remember. We live in the world, and we recall the world, and one day we won't do either anymore. The church bells will ring and the drunks will drink. A mother will bring her cow to pasture and tell the other women that she once had a son

---

*No question that Tolstoy loved the man, but he says contradictory things about Chekhov's work, including once whispering to Chekhov directly that his plays were "worse" than those of Shakespeare, a writer Tolstoy didn't much care for. Elsewhere in his personal correspondence he says nobody compares to Chekhov.

who was a bishop. She'll say this timidly, afraid that she may not be believed.

And indeed there were some who did not believe her.

As I've been taking these notes, the two gossiping doctors have been replaced by a couple of much quieter nurses. One is reading the *San Francisco Examiner*. A moment ago, she began to read to her friend from the obituaries. "Glenda Hildebidle was ninety-seven. It says her parents preceded her in death. You think!"

"There must have been no next of kin. They had to write something."

"Right, no husband, kids, et cetera."

"The obit writer figured Glenda must have had parents."

"Stands to reason."

"Does, doesn't it? And now look, they've made the paper."

• • •

A BACHELOR UNCLE

Call this a Chicago story. It's true, though I've never understood why this matters so much. It seems a cheap way of looking at a story, to judge it by whether or not it actually happened. For me, all stories are fiction. The only question is: Does it rattle the soul or not?

We had a bachelor uncle, Uncle Harry, and my brother and I loved him. He wasn't really our uncle. He was my grandmother's first cousin. She always said she'd never had much use for the man herself, but, my grandmother said, we were the only family Harry had. He'd materialize sometimes, with much fanfare, on holidays.

I think of Uncle Harry bursting through the back door of my grandparents' house on Pine Point Drive (nobody ever used the back door of that house; nobody even knew where it was beneath all that ivy) in a wet trench coat, rain pouring down from the brim of his hat to the kitchen floor, shouting, "Hallo! Hallo! Anybody ashore?" My brother and I would sprint to the kitchen, and Uncle Harry would kneel down and offer up his nose. "Honk the schnozz, go ahead and honk it!" A monster of a nose, flabby and riddled with poppy seeds, and when we squeezed his nostrils together, he'd honk like a frantic goose. I've heard geese since who had nothing on Harry.

So my brother and I loved him, though we got the gist from the rest of the family that he was a half-drunk loser who worked in the post office, the one above Congress Parkway. Can you imagine? A member of our (theoretically) illustrious family is a postal clerk? And not at the window, either. Uncle Harry worked in the back. He sorted mail, stacked packages. A nearly seventy-year-old man lifts boxes for a living? According to my banker grandfather, Uncle Harry was also a card-carrying socialist of the "Emma Goldman type," by which he meant that Harry not only had rabble-rouser tendencies, he was a Jew with rabble-rouser tendencies, which was a different kettle of fish altogether, and especially outrageous given all the bounty this country has shared with our people.

"Emma Goldman was an anarchist," my brother pointed out once.

My grandfather: "I'll anarchist your ass."

But it is true that when Harry did come to us out of the night, standing there bundled up in the kitchen, in his hat, he often did give a diatribe on the day's news from a leftist perspective. "Unelected Jerry Ford pardons Tricky Dick for the health of the country? If we're that sick, we're already dead."

"And you on the government dime. Taking a bite right out of the hand—"

"Harry, it's Thanksgiving," my grandmother said, "why don't you take off your coat and stay a while?" which was her way of saying exactly the opposite.

And he never did stay a while, and he never did take off his coat.

As far as I can remember, Harry never did step past the kitchen of that rambling, cavernous house on Pine Point Drive. Encouraging Harry to stay was the best way to get rid of him. That, and my grandfather not so discreetly slipping him a few dollars. My grand-mother said this was the only reason he came to visit us in the first place. Money in his pocket, he'd vanish again into the rain.

We were the only family he had.

Every time I drive under the old post office on Congress—it still looms above the road like a weary prison—I think of him. Of Harry exploding through the back door bearing rain in his hat. Once he threw me up in the air and my head hit the kitchen ceiling. My grandmother shouted, "You'll break his neck!"

Things happened. There was my grandfather's near-bankruptcy. My parents split up. There was my aunt's serious illness. What was left of my small family was pulled in different directions, and there were fewer and fewer occasions for all of us to get together on Pine Point Drive. Finally, my grandparents were forced to sell that house. Years piled up, a decade, a decade and a half. My brother called me from college. He'd ignored me for a few years, but every once in a while he remembered me. I was a junior in high school.

"Hey, whatever happened to Harry?" Eric said.

"Harry who?"

"Uncle Harry. How many Harrys—"

"He's at the post office," I said. "Where else would he be?"

"He'd be eighty-something, at least."

"Maybe he's dead."

"But wouldn't we have heard? Wouldn't there have been a funeral?"

I rode my bike over to my father's house, the house I grew up in, the house we decamped from when my mother decided she couldn't live with my father a minute longer. *Keep the house*, my mother had said. *I'll take the kids. I just want out of here, all right?* It was the '8os. Things were different.

"Harry?" my father said. "That's an easy one. Harry's dead."

"How do you know?"

My father went silent, a rare thing. We were in the kitchen at the small round table that was always too small for the four of us. When we ate, our knees used to touch. I always wondered why my parents didn't buy a bigger table. And my father and I sat at our old kitchen table and tried to pretend nobody was missing. At that moment it was less about an uncle who wasn't even an uncle, a man we used to see at most once or twice a year, anyway, than about my mother and my brother—and yet, still, where was Harry? If he was dead, wouldn't we—

"I have no idea how I know," my father said.

My grandparents didn't know, either. They couldn't remember the last time they'd heard from him. By then my aunt, their daughter, was so sick they had no grief left to spare.

Nobody in the family even had a phone number for the man. Harry would either show up on holidays or he wouldn't, and when he did, like I say, he never stayed long.

That year I happened to be an intrepid high school reporter. It was me, Peter Maxwell Orner, who broke the story that our local hot dog place, Nathan's, was being forced (under threat!) to change its name by an evil empire of a hot dog corporation from New York City. And so I became obsessed—for a while, anyway—with finding my uncle Harry.

I checked with the post office. He'd retired in 1982. I checked his last known address, a small apartment on Irving Park Road and Clark. He'd moved out that same year, 1982, and hadn't left any forwarding address. For years his mail had been returned to sender. A neighbor did tell me that she remembered Harry, but that it was rare that you were in the hall with him at the same time. "You know how it is," she said. "Maybe he'd wait to come out until there were no more footsteps. Some are like that." I remember how much this surprised me at the time. He'd always been so garrulous with us.

I checked hospitals, nursing homes, cemeteries. I learned that the Cook County morgue stores hundreds of unclaimed bodies every year and that pauper burials happen across the city nearly each day. Chicago is, of course, vast beyond imagination, and I wasn't a very good reporter. Mostly I just drove around the city sharing joints with my friend Marcus Boz in my mother's Corolla. Marcus would see a man on a corner, say, at the intersection of Clybourne and Van Buren, and he'd shout: "Sir, excuse me, but are you, or are you not, the enigmatic Uncle Harry formerly of the U.S. Postal Service?"

What's true about this story is not only that it happened—somewhere along the line, my family lost track of Uncle Harry—but that even after we discovered he'd disappeared, it didn't especially shake us up. It became, after a while, almost normal, run-of-the-mill, to lose someone in this way, even one of our own. Eric and I still say: *Call once in a while; don't go pulling a Harry on me.*

Here's what I think now. He was a man who, according to my grandfather, never left the city of Chicago. He'd been too old for World War II, and even if he had been called up, he probably would have found a way out of it, Harry being a pacifist (which went hand in hand, my grandfather said, with his otherwise pinko nature). But I wonder if he didn't, in the end, wander away to die in some new place. Somewhere he might have been even more anonymous than he was in his own city. In the 1980s you could still drop off the face of the earth, or at least out of Chicago. It's almost a comfort to think about. To be so out of reach even the debt collectors and their databases can't smoke you out. If Harry owes somebody money, which I'm sure he does, then they'll probably find his bones somewhere, someday. This might have made the old man in the wet trench coat laugh.

There is something graceful about simply walking away. I think of Uncle Harry in Rockford, Joliet, Peoria, or maybe across the Mississippi River in Muscatine, Iowa. After roaming an unfamiliar city for a few days, ruminating on all the empty storefronts, all that life sucked away, he spends the last of his money doing some laundry before going back to a semi-furnished room. In my memory of him he was a jolly fat man. It's possible he was, but then again, he never took his coat off, so maybe he was thinner underneath than he always seemed. He lies, in Muscatine or Peoria, on a bed with his shoes on, and waits.

The Stories of Breece DJ Pancake

Foreword by James Alan McPherson   Afterword by John Casey

WINTER IN SEPTEMBER

Stories fail if you read them only once. You've got to meet a story again and again, in different moods, in different eras of your life. This morning, in Bolinas, a town on a peninsula on the western edge of the continent, I went back—again—to the little kitchen of a farmhouse in West Virginia.

Why a Breece D'J Pancake story this morning? I only know I woke up early and searched the shelves of this cabin where I spend the other half of my life for something that would slow me down and knock me flat. It also might be that I needed, this morning, some kind of fictional anodyne because I've been thinking about my father. His hold on this world seems to be loosening. I see him now, in Chicago, in front of the television, every hour becoming more and more the same. My father in retreat. Surprising for such a relentless, raging man, a man who used to get up—late, always late, my father likes his sleep—and still feel the need to conquer every day of every year.

I've always resisted the notion of fiction as consolation. I've always seen it as something that is supposed to disrupt my life, to shake me out of treacherous contentment—but there are days, mornings like these, when it does provide a little solace, when reality itself, whatever this actually is, gets to be more than I can take. So this morning I read "First Day of Winter" slowly, the September sun hardly up, the cabin silent but for the churn of this ancient refrigerator. When I finished, I put the book down on the kitchen table and went outside for a while. A cold dawn in Bolinas, and I wished we had snow here like they do in West Virginia or in Chicago, but the wind in the trees was enough, and I thought about Hollis and his parents, his half-mad mother, his blind old father. Hollis is trying to keep his family together even though he knows the farm won't sustain them much longer. And winter's coming. Another long winter is coming.

> The sun was blackened with snow, and the valley closed in
> quietly with humming, quietly as an hour of prayer.

Pancake listened to the silence between his characters and also to the silence between sentences, between words. "First Day of Winter" is short, at least in terms of pages. It took me about an hour to read and read it again. It felt, in the best of senses, exactly like this: an hour of prayer.

The story is about aging, about responsibility. It is about the people we spend our lives living with, worrying over, only to find that when it comes down to it, we hardly know them at all. I've come to the tentative conclusion that the people we know best become—remain?—mysteries to us to the end. Our lack of knowledge doesn't mean we don't love them. Maybe it's the mystery that sustains the love, is the love.

* * *

I once read that a reader is a person who lacks a critic's complacency. I've always strived to be an uncomplacent reader, to retain a sense of wonder, even for stories I've read a dozen times. Sometimes I read a story and I think about it for hours, days, or, if I'm lucky, years. The thinking is the thing. The most I can give back to any story is a silence born of awe. But there are times, like these, when you want to say something, anything, if only to yourself and the wind in the trees.

The writer killed himself before his twenty-seventh birthday in 1979. He never lived to hold his own book in his hands. I wonder if it would have made a difference, if it might have made him pause. I doubt it. Wonderful as books are, they can't talk, can't hold us in their arms, and can't whisper us out of an early so long, either. And yet "First Day of Winter" is one of those stories that might have the power to save someone, if not the person who wrote it. What's beautiful and wrenching is that there is no resolution. What will happen to this old mother and father? Will they leave the farm? We'll never know. You don't come to a story like this for answers. Think of "First Day of Winter" as you might an old, trusted friend, the sort of friend who offers no glib, false sense of hope, just a quiet fortitude.

Read "First Day of Winter" fast and you'll miss everything. You might shrug: *That's all?* Read it slowly and you'll stay up all night with Hollis. You'll watch him watching his own reflection in the glass of the window as he worries about the farm's debts, the bank, the slaughter that's already gone to market and won't fetch decent prices, the corn that's been reduced to stubble in the fields. And in the morning, likewise exhausted, you, too, will descend the stairs alongside Hollis. His parents, long since awake, are waiting in the kitchen. The coffee was made so long ago it has gone stone cold.

His mother would not bathe and the warm kitchen smelled of her as she sat eating oatmeal with his father. The lids of the blind man's eyes hung half closed and he had not combed his hair; it stuck out in tufts where he had slept on it.

These sentences ache. Writers so often restrain themselves from trying to show what love truly looks like in practice, out of justifiable fear that it might get sentimental and therefore meaningless. But I wonder if our concern about what's sentimental isn't actually a manifestation of our sentimentality. We can't show what love feels like without embarrassment, and so we avoid the attempt altogether. Is this how it is out here in our lives? In our beds? Our kitchens? Don't we, also, mourn our losses before they are even lost? Tell me that isn't sentimental. Pancake's depiction of love is fearless. Hollis looks so closely at his father's uncombed hair. He can hardly contain himself, and so of course he does what any other loving son would do. He flees that kitchen.

> "I've got to go work on the car," Hollis said, and went toward the door.
> "Car's been sitting too long," the old woman yelled. "You be careful of snakes."

Not long after, as Hollis is outside examining the cracked engine block, the father shuffles outside with his cane to offer unwanted advice.

> "You can tell she's locking up." The blind man faced him.
> "This ain't a tractor."

When I took the book off the shelf this morning, I thought of how little Pancake's characters say to each other, how much silence pervades this work. Rereading, I found I was wrong. His people talk more to each other than I'd remembered. Yet because the dialogue—this word sounds clinical here, call it talk—is so intrinsic to the landscape of the story, you don't notice it as a separate entity.

> In the faded morning the land looked scarred. The first snows had already come, melted, sealed the hills with a heavy frost the sun could not soften. Cold winds had peeled away the last clinging oak leaves, left the hills a quiet gray-brown that sloped into the valley on either side.
> He saw the old man's hair bending in the wind.
> "Come on inside, you'll catch cold."
> "You going hunting like I asked?"

I remember a painting I once saw in a museum. A mother, a father, and a child huddled together on a beach, in the wind, their clothes flapping. There is something so vulnerable about a family of three. Take one away and what's left but a permanently empty space the other two must carry? I think of this heart-crushing painting now as I think about the three in this story. As I think about my daughter and her mother. We are three also. And as I think about my own father half asleep in front of the television. My brain flings all over the map. I'm in Northern California reading about a family in West Virginia, feeling guilty that the last time I was back home in Chicago, I didn't even take the time to go and see my father.

It gets me every time. The way a story about characters, nonexistent people, pushes us back to our own, the people who do exist, who do walk the earth. In such a brief life, Breece Pancake gave us so much. It feels greedy to ask for more. And yet what about him? What about all the characters—people—Pancake never gave himself the chance to create? Wouldn't they have been a solace to him?

* * *

Hollis comes home with a bag full of squirrels for dinner. Over the meal, he tells his parents that he's trying to get Jake, his pastor brother, to take the two of them in, that it's time, that they can't hold out like this any longer. His father tries to protest, but can't come up with any words. He breaks down and weeps. Minutes pass. Nobody speaks.

> The old man was still crying, and she went to him, helped him from the chair. He was bent with age, with crying, and he raised himself slowly, strung his flabby arm around the woman's waist.

After dinner Hollis lies down on the couch and tries—again— to sleep. He listens to the cattle lowing to be fed. His mother softly hums as his father cries in his sleep. A fragile family makes it across another day.

John Edgar Wideman
WINNER OF THE PEN/Faulkner

all stories are true

WIDEMAN'S WELCOME

Other stories cut so close you can tell them only in shards. Try taking on the whole thing directly and it only breaks apart on the page. You can't talk about it. You've got to talk about it. You can't talk about it.

A few years ago I was away from my daughter for five weeks. She was about two and a half at the time, and I remember sitting in a little coffee shop in upstate New York feeling rested, and guilty for all the time I was spending by myself. I took out John Edgar Wideman's *All Stories Are True*. I often carry this collection around with me. The energy of Wideman's prose is like a shot of epinephrine. And his work always reminds me to get my head out of my own sand and look around. I began to reread the last story in the collection, "Welcome." By the first sentence of the second paragraph—"She would be twelve now"—I realized I wasn't going to be able to finish it this time. My family would be surprised to hear that I cry. They've never seen me do it. I do it down in the garage, tearlessly. There's this welling up and I have to gulp air because I feel like I'm suffocating. I hide my face (from myself) in a book.

I think of the first line of Ford Madox Ford's *The Good Soldier*. *This is the saddest story I have ever heard.*

Out of many contenders, the saddest story I have ever heard (and reading, I believe, is a way of listening) is, by a wide margin, Wideman's "Welcome." That day in Essex, New York, in a coffee shop called the Pink Pig, I picked up a *People* instead. No big deal. How many greater challenges have I shirked? But I remember my cowardice. I couldn't endure someone else's losses on the page because I was too busy missing my own people. What does this say about my ability to endure my own losses when those losses inevitably come? As they have, as they will again. This morning, as an act of private penance, my family asleep, I returned to "Welcome" and wept. All-out wept for a change. For two lost children in a story, Njeri and Will.

It's the end of December, Christmastime—Homewood, Pittsburgh. The streets are covered with the rags and tags of snow, and the wind, known as "the hawk," blows under your clothes the moment you step outside—but still the carolers sing. And one family is grieving for its missing children. Sis lost her daughter—Njeri—at just over a year old. It happened a few Decembers back, but the pain is ever-present, especially this time of year. Tom has lost a teenage son to prison—a life sentence. Both losses are unassuageable and infinite.

> You could lose a child like that, once and for always in an instant and walk around forever with a lump in your throat, with the question of *what might have been* weighing you down every time you measure the happiness in someone else's face. Or you could lose a child and have him at the same time and how did this other way of losing a child in prison for life change her brother.

Separate calamities, yet in this family grief merges. The story is told mostly from the point of view of Sis. Here she is talking on the phone with her mother about Tom before he arrives home. Her mother begins: "After all that's happened these past few years, it's a wonder he's not crazy."

> Wonder we're not all stone crazy.
> Sometimes I believe we're being tested.
> Well, I wish whoever's conducting the damned test would get it the hell over with. Enough's enough.
> You sound like him now.
> He's my brother.

As Sis walks the winter sidewalks on her way to buy groceries, the faces and voices of her family—the living, the dead, the gone—flood her mind. The story moves forward deep inside Sis's consciousness, with few intrusive transitions. For Wideman, thought and time refuse to be linear. They bob and flow like the unpredictable current of memory itself. The story captures, as few I know, the crazy ebb and flow of an ordinary day: as we carry our groceries, as we lug our devastations.

> Doctor said there's nothing else we can do, Mrs. Crawford. I'm sorry, Mrs. Crawford. And he was. A sorry-ass bringer of bad news and nothing else he could do. Nobody to blame. Just that sorry moment when he said Njeri had to die and nobody's fault nobody could do anything more and because he was sorry there in front of her bringing the sorry news why shouldn't she strike him down tear up his sorry white ass just because there was nothing else she could do nobody could do nobody to blame just knock him down and stomp on his chest and grind those coke bottle glasses into his soft sorry face.

At its starkest "Welcome" is about how we survive the unsurvivable. Tom arrives in Pittsburgh for Christmas Eve. The family is reunited for a brief time, and all the love and absence crowd together. Nothing aches more at a gathering of family than when someone who should be there—isn't. It's like there's a gaping hole in the room. Everybody has to step around it. And when Sis does manage to talk to Tom alone, he tells her how hard it is to come home, to face these familiar streets. On the one hand, it's rejuvenating, but at the same time, given what he's going through, it's a kind of living hell.

> Like the world is washed fresh after rain, right, and when you step out in the sunshine everything is different, Sis, anything seems possible, well, think of just the opposite.

And then—and here's the part I anticipated not being able to take that day in the coffee shop—this story takes a sharp and magnificent swerve outward into other people. "Welcome" is told, as I said, from mostly the perspective of Sis, but Wideman won't be constrained by any conventional notion about point of view. As the grief merges, so do the voices of these two siblings. Sis and Tom become one as Tom recounts how the night before, after his flight arrived, he drove over to his old favorite place, the Woodside Barbeque, for some chicken wings. "You know how I love them salty and greasy as they are I slap on extra sauce and pop a cold Iron City." On the way, Tom tells Sis, who tells us, he sees a young father and his little boy waiting for a bus in the cold. The bus isn't coming for hours, if at all, this late on a weekend.

> ... and I think Damn why are they out there in this arctic-ass weather, the kid shivering and crying in a skimpy K Mart snowsuit, the man not dressed for winter either, a hooded

sweatshirt under his shiny baseball jacket and I see a woman somewhere, the mother, another kid really, already split from this young guy, a broken home, the guy's returning the boy to his mother, or her mother or his and this is the only way, the best he can do and the wind howls the night gets blacker and blacker . . .

What follows in the story is a moment of such rare grace it hurts. I've returned to it many times just to watch it happen again. I don't want to get into what it might have taken John Edgar Wideman, the man, the father of a son in prison, to write this story, to create such music. This is the gift of fiction. Out of his own agony, Wideman grants his fictional father, Tom, his fictional mother, Sis—and the rest of us—deliverance from our pain.

On my way back past that same corner I see the father lift his son and hug him. No bus in sight and it's still blue cold but the kid's not fidgeting and crying anymore he's up in his daddy's arms and I think Fuck it. They'll make it. Or if they don't somebody else will come along and try. Or somebody else try. To make kids. A home. A life. That's all we can do. Any of us.

Because all our losses are collective. If they're not, we're truly doomed. If we can't overcome them ourselves, the very least we can do is recognize that we aren't the only ones out here trying to get by.

Frank O'Connor

The Lonely Voice

A Study of the Short Story

Introduction by Russell Banks

THE LONELY VOICE

Frank O'Connor's *The Lonely Voice*, first published in 1963, is one of the few books about short stories (or writing in general*) I've ever been able to stomach much. This is because O'Connor never offers any insight on *how* to tell stories. O'Connor knows such thoughts would not only be useless, they would completely defeat his purpose. Stories are patently abnormal things; each one a warped and unique universe unto itself. The minute you attempt to streamline a certain methodology of telling, you put an artificial limitation on the expression of human experience. That was a mouthful. Put it like this: Stories can't be caged.

The Lonely Voice is about storywriters O'Connor reveres: Maupassant, Chekhov, Turgenev, Joyce, Mary Lavin, J. F. Powers; and a couple he doesn't: Hemingway (innovative style triumphs over substance) and Katherine Mansfield (brilliant but forgettable). It's about the idea of being a storywriter itself, this lunatic idea of devoting your life's blood to making up stories about

*Another is Italo Calvino's *Six Memos for the Next Millennium*.

things that never happened and people who never existed. It's an imperfect, provocative, cranky book (among other things, his thoughts on Hemingway sweep far too broadly and he's way off on Mansfield), and I couldn't live without it. I've taped *The Lonely Voice* back together so many times now the pages are all out of order.

> For the short-story writer there is no such thing as essential form. Because his frame of reference can never be the totality of a human life, he must be forever selecting the point at which he can approach it, and each selection he makes contains the possibility of a new form as well as the possibility of a complete fiasco.

I once tried to get all that tattooed on my chest, but the artist said he didn't do paragraphs. I don't know about you, but I am constantly dancing, flat-footedly, between two poles—moderate success and complete fiasco—in writing and, God knows, in life, though often, as you can probably tell by now, I am unable to separate the two.

The Lonely Voice is also a lamentation for stories never imagined. O'Connor speaks up for stories and the people who write them—and in doing so, the people who read them—as few ever have. Another sentence that amounts to prophesy:

> The saddest thing about the short story is the eagerness with which those who write it best try to escape it.

Even today, fifty years later, for most fiction writers, and certainly for most publishers, the novel, hell or high water, remains supreme, especially in this country where we still revere thick for thick's sake. This has always confounded me. I'm with O'Connor.

Chekhov's example is not enough? What about Welty, whose greatest work is in the story? Mavis Gallant, anybody? Grace Paley? Andre Dubus? Where's the mighty Borges novel? Borges, who once said: I like beginnings and I like endings and I leave the long middles to Henry James. To this, I say, Hallelujah. How many good stories have been lost because writers slaved away their best years larding unnecessary words onto a story that never needed them? What truths buried? What new forms never created?

> There is in the short story at its most characteristic something we do not find in the novel—an intense awareness of human loneliness.

If the novel is the more communal form, the short story is for loners, for those off to the side. Or to put it more mundanely, stories are like me at a party. I hover near the appetizers and have been known to consume entire wheels of cheese in order to keep busy. Anything to avoid the oppressive mob laughter of group conversations.

O'Connor believed that one of the reasons stories stand apart is that so many great ones are told from the perspective of an outsider or, as he put it, "in the voice of a member of a submerged population." He acknowledged the clunkiness of the term, but admitted he couldn't come up with anything better. Members of a submerged population are people who, for whatever reason, either by force or by choice, have been excluded from what might be called majority society. Often they are people without material, political, or social influence. To illustrate his point, O'Connor recalls Ivan Turgenev's line about all Russian writers having emerged from under Nikolai Gogol's "The Overcoat." Gogol, arguably, was among the first writers to thrust a true nobody, a common clerk, into a starring role.

And so, *in a certain department there served a certain clerk*; a not very remarkable clerk, one might say—short, somewhat pockmarked, somewhat red-haired, even with a somewhat nearsighted look, slightly bald in front, with wrinkles on both cheeks and a complexion that is known as hemorrhoidal.

Gogol takes Cervantes's Don Quixote and makes him even more ridiculous, more isolated—and far more forlorn. Don Quixote has a house and a library back home, servants, his trusty horse—and, of course, Sancho Panza.

Akaky Akakievich has a coat.

You know him (he may be you) and you know the story even if you've never come across the text yourself. "The Overcoat" is the rare piece of fiction that so captures what it's like to be powerless in an inhumane society that it has sunk into our consciousness through battalions of writers who have come after it, Russian or otherwise. This is what Turgenev meant. Generations of writers have carried Akaky Akakievich on their backs. Melville's Bartleby is a quieter brother. Gogol's clerk reaches out (for his beloved coat) across a century and a half, across the border of language itself.

A poor man, a petty, abused bureaucrat, is able, due to an unexpected windfall, to purchase a new overcoat from a tailor. You know how it is with new things. I've had a couple of new cars in my life. Not new new cars, used new cars, very used new cars, but still, a new car is a new car. I remember how I felt those first few days driving those cars. Like I was newly born. Like now, at last, I had my whole life ahead of me, now that I had a Subaru with under a hundred thousand miles and a dented left fender.

Watch Akaky Akakievich as he struts away from Petrovich the tailor's house and into the St. Petersburg chill.

Meanwhile, Akaky Akakievich walked on in the most festive disposition of all his feelings. At each instant of every minute he felt there was a new overcoat on his shoulders, and several times he even smiled from inner satisfaction. . . . He did not notice the road at all . . .

But that very night, as he's floating home from a party (hosted by his office mates in mock celebration of his new coat), a gang of "people with mustaches" pull the coat right off his back. Less than half a sentence and it's over, the coat's history. The theft changes everything, and for the first time in his life the clerk is motivated to stand up for himself. He takes definitive action. First he goes to the police. After getting no satisfaction there, Akaky Akakievich marches, through the cold, in his tattered "house coat," to visit a certain important person, a general, to request that the full weight of the government assist in recovering his new overcoat. The whole thing is ludicrous. Before Akaky has even arrived in the general's office, Gogol has skewered him (and the system) so hilariously it's impossible to take any of it seriously.

It should be realized that this *certain important person* had become an important person only recently, and till then had been an unimportant person. However, his position even now was not considered important in comparison with other, still more important ones. But there will always be found a circle of people for whom something unimportant in the eyes of others is already important. He tried, however, to increase his importance by many other means—namely, he introduced the custom of lower clerks meeting him on the stairs when he came to the office; of no one daring to come to him directly, but everything in the strictest order: a collegiate registrar should report to a provincial secretary, a provincial secretary to a titular or whatever else, and in this fashion the case should reach him. . . . The chief principle of his system was strictness. "Strictness, strictness, and—strictness," he used to say, and with the last word usually looked importantly into the face of the person he was addressing.

Still, I can't help reading the scene straight. Akaky Akakievich genuinely believes that the general could find his coat, if only he would try. The general immediately sends him packing.

"Do you not know the order? What are you doing here? Do you not know how cases are conducted? You ought to have filed a petition about it in the chancellery; it would pass to the chief clerk, to the section chief, then be conveyed to my secretary, and my secretary . . ."

Eventually, it is no exaggeration to say, the loss of the coat kills the clerk. After walking home from the general's office, he catches a severe cold and the next day is found to have a high fever. He's done for. But this is Akaky Akakievich's moment—he'll be forever etched—and even death itself won't quiet him now.

Certain books, we are told, capture the zeitgeist of a time and place. It seems to me that this idea is an easy way for the majority population or, more accurately, those who claim to speak for it to pretend to understand itself. Forget the zeitgeist. I don't believe there is any. Because a given society's profoundest stories always speak from the margins. Think of the stories you most revere. Do they reaffirm the status quo or puncture it irrevocably? There is no zeitgeist in Gogol's overcoat other than the zeitgeist of a single trampled-upon human being. If every bureaucrat in every government agency or corporate office was required to read "The Overcoat" once a month, so-called common people might have a chance to forge a more human relationship with power. But that's the joke, right? Power rarely pauses to listen, much less read. Why should it? Even the narrator of this very story can't help laughing at the man.

> At last poor Akaky Akakievich gave up the ghost. Neither his room nor his belongings were sealed, because, first, there were no heirs, and, second, there was very little inheritance left—namely, a bunch of goose quills, a stack of white official paper, three pairs of socks, two or three buttons torn off of trousers, and the housecoat already familiar to the reader. To whom all this went, God knows: that, I confess, did not even interest the narrator of this story.

Akaky Akakievich represents nobody but his own bones. The little man, the nobody, in spite of degradation, humiliation, even the grave (what's more an insult than a cold hole in the ground?), will rise up from six feet under and carry on his search for a coat that not only once kept him warm but that also, and this is essential, gave him dignity. Around Kalinkin Bridge, a dead man is said to be violently yanking coats off shoulders and causing horror and consternation among the populace, including a certain *important person*. But even more affecting is how one lonely voice will haunt the memory of one unnamed fellow clerk, a man who had once abused Akaky and is now ashamed. It's a line Akaky Akakievich never said out loud himself because he never knew how to say it. But the truth was always there.

> "I am your brother."

But back to the question: Why a short story? Why Frank O'Connor's insistence that there is something different about this form? Why not *The Overcoat: A Novel*? It's not that he wasn't capable. Gogol's *Dead Souls* is one of the more insane masterpieces that exist in novel form. But my thought is that a novel version of Akaky might have tempted Gogol to offer up some kind of closure for this story. And for Akaky Akakievich there can be no closure. Every time I read the story I feel the loss of that coat down to my feet. After the last period, I fall and keep on falling. Our most enduring short stories never end. In this way, they may last even longer than their fatter counterparts. Another way of saying it: The difference between a short story and a novel is the difference between an inarticulate pang in your heart compared to the tragedy of your whole life. There are so many things we find it impossible to say. But we, like Akaky Akakievich pleading his case to a general who doesn't hear a word he says, try to tell them, anyway. What choice? The failure of certain stories to say what they are trying to say is the source of their inexplicable force.

· · ·

*The
Diaries
of*

FRANZ KAFKA

Volume One

1910-1913

Edited by Max Brod

STRAY THOUGHTS ON KAFKA

1. Out the Window

> Whoever leads a solitary life and yet now and then feels the
> need for some kind of contact . . .
>
> —Franz Kafka, "The Street Window"

We lived in Prague that year: 1999. The place was crawling with Americans as clueless as we were. *Woo-hoo, what iron curtain?* The weather and the wet streets were romantically gloomy. Rent was cheap. We didn't need much to stay alive. We began to talk about beer like scholars. And there were the *antikvariats*, the used bookstores. These dusty nirvanas were in every neighborhood, and there was always a shelf full of books in English. They sold for nothing. Many of them dated from the war. I bought a first-edition Virginia Woolf for fifteen crowns. The storeowners had contempt for any book that wasn't in Czech. *Why would anybody want to read a book that's not in Czech?* Every day I brought home another pile of books. We worshipped Václav Havel (and often staked him out at the Café Slavia) and read a lot of Milan Kundera. Communism sounded fun as told by Kundera, at least sexually. What's a little repression in a utopia where everybody is sleeping with everybody? And the Czechs tolerated us—for a while, anyway. I got a job teaching Anglo and American law at Charles University. A few years earlier, I'd graduated from law school. Though it made my mother proud, the degree has never come in very handy except this one time when I was living in Prague with the woman who would become my wife. M (she's asked me not to use her name) was making a film about what happened to the Gypsies after the fall of communism. There was better sex back then, and also, apparently, less (overt) racism. After the wall came down, so did the inhibition of many Czechs to express their dislike of people who they didn't think were European. And the Roma, who'd lived among them for centuries, had never been considered European. It was as though people thought they'd arrived three days ago to steal everybody's purses.

The Law Faculty building at Charles University was—is—a vast hulk of a structure that squats on the bank of the Vltava River. Everything about the place is unnecessarily huge, the height of the ceilings, the doors, especially the doors. I'd never seen such needlessly enormous doors. You had to yank them open with two hands. Franz Kafka studied at the Law Faculty and graduated in 1906. I was sure the place hadn't been renovated since. It wasn't hard for me to imagine him wandering those halls not built to human scale.

I had a lot of time to wander myself. The job turned out to be not very taxing. Having slogged through law school, I knew a little something about American law, but in the beginning, in any case, I didn't know what "Anglo" law even meant. WASPY? I was paid something like forty cents an hour, but again, it was enough to live on. Showing up to teach seemed optional. All the other professors had other day jobs. Capitalism was beginning to roar. But the Law

Faculty was still mired in the old days. Sometimes I had five or six students; other times it was just me and this one guy named Jan. Jan wasn't interested in Anglo or American law. He had a cousin who lived in East Lansing and wanted to practice his English without having to pay a private tutor.

This is nothing new. A lot of people pass through Prague and dream up some dopey kinship with Kafka, but I took the fact that not only was everything I did irrelevant and completely ineffectual, I was also serving time in the *very same building where he, too, once toiled*. I thought: I am as lost here on the face of the earth as he was.

After about a year and a half, the film finished, M and I left Prague and moved to Cincinnati. Why? I'm still not sure. But doesn't everybody, at some point or another, move to their own private Cincinnati? After Cincinnati, we fled to California. Eventually, years later, we got married. Then everything fell apart. Doesn't everything always fall apart in California?

What follows is an aside, the reasons for which I hope will become clearer in a moment. Cut to that time not long after my marriage collapsed. I found myself lonely, bewildered, and, above all, exhausted. So I decided that what I really needed was a weekend at what people used to call a nudist colony but are now, in California, called clothing-optional retreats. If there is an almighty, omnipotent God, even He wouldn't have known what the hell I was thinking. Though I told myself all I wanted to do was to be alone for a while, I must have been hoping to meet someone. Why else would I have gone to a nudist colony? The minute I arrived at the place (which has since burned to the ground) I knew the whole mission, whatever my motivation, was turning out to be one of my more harebrained ideas. The less people were wearing, the more shell-shocked I generally became. After the long drive and being stuck in that place for at least a night, and needing, right away, to get away from all that competitively exposed flesh (only in America could clothing optional turn into one-upmanship), I hightailed it, fully clothed, up to the top of a mountain, where I found a thatched hut with two yoga mats side by romantic side. The hut was new, but built to look weathered and authentic. Good a place as any. I decided to hunker down on a yoga mat. I stretched out on the mat and did a few moves I thought resembled yoga before cursing myself for not bringing a book up here. Or at least some drugs. Or a shotgun. I stared up at the roof of my hut. I tried to will a sense of quietude amid the redwoods. I sat cross-legged and tried to imitate meditation. That didn't work, either. Too much peace makes me nervous. I must have been up there for at least an hour, staring at the thatch, ruminating on the multiplying effects of failure, when I was joined by a chatty, bearded guy wearing nothing but hiking boots and a loose thong.

Excuse me, bro, but what's with all the threads?

Little chilly, that's all. Must be the altitude.

You want to process this? Clothes are a construct, a prison. You unhappy in your own skin? Is that it, bro? Why deny the gift?

That's it, exactly. Unhappy but happy. Unhappily happy?

So yeah, as much as I wanted to bludgeon the guy with my yoga mat, I was also grateful to him, because as much as I'd told myself I wanted it, needed it, solitude is not only scary, it's work. As long as this thonged nudist was there to loathe, I didn't have to be with myself. Which was becoming draining. I guess what I'm getting at is that true loneliness is a rare and difficult thing. We want it. We don't want it at all.

Maybe it's always been this way. Here's an utterly unprovable theory I've been developing over the past couple of hours concerning Franz Kafka, after reading haphazard bits of his diary. He often craved it, but the reality is that the man wasn't lonely at all. His social life was demanding and often extraordinarily busy. I'm lucky if I get invited to three parties a year, and the last one I truly enjoyed was a fund-raiser for Obama back in 2008. This was only a few months after my foray into the world of clothing optional. There, at the house of a young, indescribably rich couple, I met the mother of my daughter. Actually, we'd met before, but she hadn't returned my e-mails. She's a novelist, but that night was a volunteer bartender and as liberal with the vodka as she is in her politics. I hovered by the bar and downed vodka tonics like a hero for Obama. Yes, we can. *Sí, se puede.* Somehow, together, we wobbled back to her apartment on Precita Park. Later, not that same night, we created a child. This took us both by surprise, although biologically it shouldn't have. Biologically it was perfectly logical. We all know how this goes, but it still amazes me: together we created a big-eyed kid. In between, there was love and a fat, lazy dog.

But Kafka? We're talking about a guy who was out at the Café Louvre yukking it up with Max Brod and his other law school buddies *all the time.* He often read his stories out loud to the howling laughter of his friends. Kafka was a serial fiancé who never married. He was a man who ran *to* people as obsessively as he ran away from them. My thought (it is now late dusk, the kitchen has changed colors, and I haven't turned on the light yet) is that Kafka wrote so much about loneliness because he could never make up his mind whether he wanted it or not. In his diary he writes:

One can never be alone enough when one writes, why even night is not night enough.

And:

I have no family feeling and visitors make me almost feel as though I were being maliciously attacked. Being alone has a power over me that never fails.

But there's also:

> I passed by the brothel as though past the house of a beloved.

And:

> It seems so dreadful to be a bachelor, to become an old man struggling to keep one's dignity while begging for an invitation whenever one wants to spend an evening in company.

We are the sum of our contradictions. How could it be otherwise? Still, this fundamental and unanswerable and lingering question: Alone or with other people?

Many of Kafka's stories involve a struggle between a craving for loneliness and a terror of it. See "The Judgment," written in a single feverish night. Why the hullabaloo over an imaginary Russian friend? Either invite him to the wedding or don't . . .

But there's one very short piece that unfolds, unambiguously, in the motion of a single paragraph, like a fist opening. It's called "The Street Window" and was completed not long after Kafka's graduation from law school. All a lone man has to do is go near a window that looks out upon a street.

> And if he is in the mood of not desiring anything and only goes to his windowsill a tired man, with eyes turning from his public to heaven and back again, now wanting to look out and having thrown his head up a little, even then the horses below will draw him down into their train of wagons and tumult, and so at last into the human harmony.

At some point, much as we talk a big game about needing to go it alone, we can't help but be pulled to the window, to the noise and the voices. Come on into my hut and tell me about the demonology of garments, thong man. I'll listen.

2. Chopping Wood

> My lung was fair at least out there, here where I've been for the last fortnight. I've not been able to see the doctor. But it can't be so bad considering for instance that I was able—holy vanity!—to chop for an hour and more without getting tired, and yet was happy, for moments.
> —Kafka, *Letters to Milena* (1917)

In the beginning his swing is wobbly, but gains a sort of clipped, if awkward, grace as he chops. It isn't because he needs wood for any stove. This is pure sport. He's a guest at a German spa. He's forty. He'll be dead of tuberculosis in seven years. But at the moment his lungs feel hardy. And he's filled with expectations. He knows that as soon as he's done he will go inside and write to Milena, his latest love, and tell her what he's been up to by the woodpile. He'll write, Well, I've been chopping some wood. Holy vanity. This from a man who would later (supposedly) beg that every trace of his life's work be obliterated.* Even he can't

---

*Borges, who usually has something relevant to say about anything, says that if Kafka was so intent on having his work destroyed, he would never have trusted the job to someone else.

help wanting an image of himself as a man chopping wood to lodge in Milena's imagination. For a moment? For a night? For good? He chops and he chops.

In her obituary of Kafka, Milena will write that Kafka was condemned to see the world with "blinding clarity." Consider the contradiction embedded in the phrase "blinding clarity." By being prevented from seeing, he sees. But right now he's just chopping wood. And as he chops, this man, Franz, is alive and in love (again), robust even. The ax squeaks like a mouse when he worries it from the log. He raises the ax again. The wood waits. He swings—then the sound, like a loud, distant, beautiful knock.

3. Possible Father

In an essay on Kafka called "The I Without the Self," W. H. Auden alludes briefly to a rumor "which, if true, might have occurred in a Kafka story." The rumor, first circulated by Max Brod, is that Kafka once fathered a son but that the mother never told him the boy existed. The child, according to Brod, died in 1921 at the age of seven. Auden concludes: "The story cannot be verified because the mother was arrested by the Germans in 1944 and never heard from again."

Let's say for the moment that it's true. Let's say that the man who knew so uncomfortably much about fathers and sons was a father himself. He just doesn't know it. At least not factually. Yet somewhere deep in his tortured psyche he has a nagging thought: *I'm somebody's father, too.* One morning, at the end of the first decade of the last century, while on his way to his office at the insurance company, in a crowded tram, he spots a boy. An ordinary-looking little boy with a round head and bushy eyebrows, but there's something familiar about him. It's the eyes. There is something too wide about them. Kafka stares at the boy and the boy stares back. Or the boy seems to, anyway. He's really only gazing, lazily, at a man in a suit, in a hat, on a packed morning tram. Other than the giveaway eyes, he's just another fat-cheeked healthy boy with not an ounce of curiosity and, most remarkably, from the point of view of his putative father, no consecrated halo of isolation. Kafka looks at the boy's feet. They aren't small. They aren't big. They are blessed average-sized feet—ordinary feet—and he thinks of them withdrawing from battered shoes at the end of a day like today and what it might be like to cradle them in his own softish hands.

4. Ceiling Dust

Decided to leave the next day. Gave notice. Stayed
nevertheless.
—Kafka, *Diary*, July 28, 1914

This was in 2006. M and I had married a year earlier, after being together almost a decade. We returned to Prague because M had received a Fulbright to study Czech film. But more to the point, we'd once been happy there. We thought living there, again, might help make us happy again. Does this ever work? To return? As if it was the place itself and not who we used to be in the place.

That last night, I waited until M was asleep, wrote a note on a piece of paper towel, and dropped it on the kitchen table. Then I lugged a hastily stuffed duffel bag two miles to my friend Hugh's apartment in Pankrác.

Hugh had been a colleague of mine at the law school back in 1999. He taught medieval legal history and was also the advisor of something called the Common Law Society, a club devoted to promoting the virtues of Anglo and American law, as well as the free market. Though I wasn't teaching that second time in

Prague (I was, as I loved to proclaim, at highbrow Fulbright gatherings, *writing a novel*), as a former visiting professor of Anglo and American law, I'd been invited to join, at Hugh's suggestion, this extracurricular organization. I attended Common Law Society meetings once a week. I listened to presentations on civil procedure, contracts, and the inherent evilness of taxation. And at some point during that year, I stood with Hugh and the students for the annual photo. Studying this picture now, a photograph that amazingly can still be found on the Web, I can see that I was dazed. With my mop of unwashed hair, I look much younger than I actually was. I'm sure that I hadn't taken a shower in days. Even so, I remember being grateful for the Common Law Society. It gave me someplace to go.

Because by then M's struggle with paranoia had become completely debilitating. Though we'd been seeking help for years, usually from psychiatrists who were more than happy to prescribe medications but rarely took much time to speak with M, before we moved back to Prague neither of us had any clue about how bad things were going to turn. And at that time I wasn't very sane myself. M and I were trapped in something I've never been able to talk about since. There are people who've known me for years who still know none of this. But it's a story, ours (my version, anyway), and at some point stories need a little light of day.

We lived in Žižkov that year, under the television tower. Sculptures of babies crawl up and down the long pillars of the tower. I used to stand on our balcony and look at those babies defying gravity. But what comes back most vividly (I wish it didn't) is how M shouted, how the smallest thing could set her off, and how embarrassed I used to get about what our Czech neighbors must think of us. Look at these Americans now, screaming their heads off. And M would become so upset with me for trying to make her be quiet—by shouting back at her, by trying to cup my hands over her mouth—that I often had to flee that apartment. I'd wander the city for hours, day and night, talking to myself, unsure of what to do. We had few friends then, and I couldn't explain to those we did have what was going on because I didn't understand it myself. This went on for months. Every morning seemed to bring a fresh catastrophe. The professors in the film department were out to get her. They were trying to sabotage her project. The landlord is screwing us out of the security deposit. *But we haven't moved out yet. How can she be screwing us over if we haven't even moved out yet?* Once, I had to knock her over in order to leave. Another time she wouldn't stop hitting herself in the face. There are other things I refuse to remember. In between there were days of calm. For instance, one weekend we went by train to a place they call Bohemian Switzerland—another place we'd once been happy. M was reading something (she always read holding the book directly up to her nose), and she laughed out loud. I asked her to read it to me. I wish I remembered what it was, but I do remember that I didn't think the line was that funny. I laughed, anyway, because I was so relieved to laugh, and I kept laughing and laughing until M said, Enough, already, it's not that funny.

Also that winter our bathtub fell through the floor of the bathroom and into our neighbor's apartment below. We came home and there was our tub in PhDr. Chroma's living room. Nobody was hurt. We laughed then, too. Even Dr. Chroma laughed. For weeks, there was a massive hole in the bathroom. When we brushed our teeth we could look down and say hello to Dr. Chroma.

Most everything else was hell. For M's increasingly frequent manic episodes, one Czech doctor recommended vitamins, and why not a kitten?

By that last night in Prague I was panicked and exhausted. The only thing I could think of to do was go home, wherever home was. I had no idea. San Francisco? Chicago? I'd never been to Hugh's apartment. Somehow, after wandering around Pankrác in the dark, I finally found the right building and pressed the buzzer. When he opened the door, Hugh didn't ask me any questions. He didn't even look that surprised to see me. Hugh was from Scotland. We weren't close friends, but sometimes he led me on long walks, tours of what he called great beheadings in Czech history. He'd point to a spot and say, Right here is where they sliced the neck of Ottar II. In this city, every corner staged a tragedy. Every square inch, Hugh would say, every building, every room—"Now, Peter, how about a coffee? Slavia or the cheap place in the library?"

That night Hugh immediately offered me his bed, the one I'd only just rousted him up from. He told me not to think twice about it, that come to think of it, he had reading to do. It was a one-room apartment. Hugh had built the sleeping loft to make room below for all his books. He said he'd built the loft too high, but that he'd become accustomed to it. He said he hoped the proximity to the ceiling wouldn't bother me very much. He said, Take the bed, I've got reading to do, really. Take the bed.

I was in such bad shape that I did. I took the man's bed.

The short night was so long. My nose touched the stucco ceiling as I tried to sleep. The ceiling was dusty. I kept wondering why the dust hadn't fallen to the floor, why it clung there to the stucco. Maybe this was why they call it stucco? I thought about this while I waited for sleep that never came. Outside Hugh's window was a highway. Tourists don't visit Pankrác. It's only famous for the prison. Václav Havel was once an inmate. In the dark I listened to the cars as they accelerated and vanished. At one point I noticed the bar of light under the bathroom door. Hugh hadn't wanted to disturb me. He'd retreated to the bathroom to read. In the lulls in the highway noise, I could hear him turning pages. In a few hours, M will wake up and read the paper towel. Kafka once wrote that writing was a form of prayer. I have no recollection of what I wrote on that paper towel, but I'd like to think it was, in some way, a prayer for us both. She'll be on her own now. And I'll leave this city for good in the morning, but this night will go on and on, still does go on and on, my nose in the dust of the ceiling.

Eudora Welty

THE BRIDE

OF THE

INNISFALLEN

By The author of The Ponder Heart

EUDORA WELTY, BADASS

This morning I woke up with a voice roaring in my ears, as if some wayward angel were talking into a bullhorn from a celestial Library of Congress: *Eudora Welty is badass. Preach to the people this incontestable gospel.*

I know, I love her, too, but listen, at the moment I'm asleep.

No, now go, shout from the mountaintops so that the people.

The people? What people?

All the people. Every single one of the people.

In any case, now I'm awake. I've had some coffee. I'm on a remote (feels remote to me, anyway) island off the coast of South Carolina, and I'm staying in a house surrounded on three sides by a salt marsh. No mountains here, and I sit with my cold coffee, watching the blue herons make footprints in the clay. I would like to enjoy this serenity for a few minutes. But this voice won't let up.

Tell the people, the people must know.

Look, seriously, who are the people you're talking about?

The people, every one of the people!

But the people know. Welty is one of America's most beloved authors. She doesn't need me or anybody else to trumpet—

Ah, see, now there it is, you condescend and call her beloved! Like she's some gentile tea-drinking biddie on a porch swing, her little legs sticking out in front of her like a cutie doll. A funny little lady who lives at the P.O. But Welty isn't anybody's favorite auntie, and you know it. She's badass, and you must tell the people—

But wait, I don't even know who the hell you even are.

I'm your inner ravings, shmuck. Who the hell do you think I am, some nut?

Oh. Well. Sorry, but I'm Weltyless at the moment. I don't have any of her books, so why don't we leave this for some other time and let me drink my—

Get thee to a library.

It's Sunday.

Oh.

Yesterday, I visited the remains of a plantation. I took the driving tour. I enjoyed the canopy of trees over the road, the loblolly pines and the palmettos, and the many birds—the pine warblers and the yellow-throated warblers—and, like a good Yankee (upon entering the South all Northerners suddenly begin referring to themselves as Yankees as though their family bled Union blue), I sat through the whole thing with a scowl, annoying my hosts and waiting for some tangible evidence of the slavery that built the place. Nice trees, nice flowers, nice birds. But where are you people hiding the truth? It came near the exit. I quote from my guidebook:

> To the right of the information kiosk, you will see the chimney
> of a slave house, the remains of one of many such dwellings

that once dotted the property. We hope you've had a pleasant visit and hope to see you again soon!!!

Maybe this is why I woke up with Welty on the brain. Often, I'm less prone to having an actual experience than I am to relating what I'm experiencing to something, anything, I've read. It's as if I don't quite exist in real time. I have a friend, a yoga teacher, who says I don't live in the present, and I say, who wants to live in the present? I looked at this lone chimney rising out of the dust and I didn't pause a moment to think, as I should have, of the generations of women who might once have cooked meals in this very spot. Instead, I thought of a Welty story called "The Burning." It was as if I needed Welty to see what I was seeing. Do you know what I mean? I needed her eyes.

(Let me come clean and add that I'm a Welty fanatic. I once made a pilgrimage to Welty's house in Jackson, Mississippi, and apparently did a good enough impersonation of a "Welty scholar" that I was permitted by the curators to handle, with surgical gloves, Welty's book collection. Or maybe they just felt sorry for me. This freak came such a long way. In any case, there, in Welty's house on Pinehurst Street, it was thrilling to hold, in my own gloved hands, her Virginia Woolfs, V. S. Pritchetts [she dearly loved Pritchett, his picture still looms above her bed] and Elizabeth Bowens, her Henry Greens, her Ross Macdonalds. I was on the hunt for scribbles in the margins. I thought I might find some previously unknown clues that might give me a hint of how she did it. I found only a few mostly unreadable notes written in faded pencil. One of them said: *Must not forget tomatoes for E.*)

* * *

It's now Monday afternoon, and from the tiny Edisto library I've picked up an old copy of Welty's last full-length, freestanding collection, *The Bride of the Innisfallen*. It was last checked out in 1981. Although the book contains some of her most innovative—call it mind-blowing—work in the short story, *The Bride of the Innisfallen* received mixed reviews when it came out. Some critics wanted her to go back to being the little lady who worked in the post office, the little lady that, even then, she never was. The stories in *The Bride of the Innisfallen* are dense and chaotic and, in the case of a story called "The Burning," also brutal and deeply disturbing. Few stories about slavery have whacked me as hard. I place "The Burning," set just after Emancipation, alongside Faulkner's *Go Down, Moses*, Morrison's *Beloved,* and Edward P. Jones's *The Known World.* In some respects, "The Burning" is even tougher to take, because it is so compressed and so immediate. There is no long view. There is no time other than *this* time. Welty captures how it feels to suddenly live in a universe utterly unlike the one you lived in the day before. What we see is what her characters see—which is, at least on a first reading, complete bedlam.

Forgive another brief aside: "The Burning" is the second story in *The Bride of the Innisfallen*. I've a long-held theory, which, like all my literary theories, is unscientific, somewhat random, and based mostly on hunch, but I believe that while authors of story collections usually put one of their best, most battle-tested stories first, they invariably put their personal favorite second. This is the story that comes closest to failure, and so the writer loves it all the more. In this instance, the opening story of *The Bride of the Innisfallen* is called "No Place for You, My Love," and it is the loneliest love story Welty ever wrote. Two strangers meet at a luncheon. They are both married. Now they're in a car heading south into the night from

New Orleans, where anything is possible. They stop at a bar. The story is so delicate, sublime even, and, finally, soaring, that anything I say in praise of it will sound hokey. Like all the words I just used. Especially "sublime." Did I just use "sublime" in public? All worthy stories are better read than talked about, but, to my mind, few more so than "No Place for You, My Love." Russell Banks once wrote you had to be forty to understand the story. I'm not sure I'd put an age requirement on it (I know a lot of old souls under ten), but I like the idea that a certain amount of experience is necessary before venturing into certain fictional domains. If I were a fascist librarian, I'd restrict readership of "No Place for You, My Love" to only those who've pursued hopeless love. It's a story where nothing happens but *everything* changes.

"The Burning," by contrast, is, I'd guess, nobody's favorite Welty story. Only the person who wrote it could truly love this orphan of a story, and only a writer as audacious as Eudora Welty would follow "No Place for You, My Love" with "The Burning," as if she meant to say, Yes, I'm of the South, and yes, I love it, yes, it is my place, but let us never, ever forget what happened on my soil.

A Union soldier on a horse rides right through the front door of a plantation house. A crowd of newly emancipated slaves follows him into the mansion. What happens next is a confusing tumult made more difficult by the fact that the story is told from a disoriented former slave's perspective. Delilah is technically free, and these soldiers, in theory anyway, have come to insure this freedom. Yet Delilah remains loyal. It's the only world she's ever known.

> It was a towering, sweating, grimacing, uneasy white horse.
> It had brought in two soldiers with red eyes and clawed,
> mosquito-racked faces—one a rider, hang-jawed and head-

hanging, and the other walking by its side, all breathing in
here now as loud as trumpets.

Miss Theo with shut eyes spoke just behind Miss Myra.
"Delilah, what is it you came in your dirty apron to tell me?"

The sisters turned with linked hands and faced the room.

"Come to tell you we got the eggs away from black broody
hen and sure enough, they's addled," said Delilah.

The Union soldiers inform the ladies that the house will be
burned, as per the orders of General Sherman. But they aren't yet,
the soldiers say, in the business of burning up people. So time to
clear out, ladies. The two sisters flatly refuse to leave. The rider gets
off the horse, hands the bridle to Delilah, and begins to chase Myra,
the younger, prettier sister, around the room. Then, right there in
the drawing room, he drops on top of her.

The story unfolds with a disquieting, seemingly comic touch,
making it all the more deadly. One thing is obvious: we're sure as
hell not at the post office. After Myra is pounced upon (it's unclear
exactly how far this assault goes), Theo, the older sister, offers Delilah to the soldiers, since she's heard Union soldiers like that sort of
thing.

> "I'm afraid you found the ladies of this house a trifle out of
> your element. My sister's the more delicate one, as you see.
> May I offer you this young kitchen Negro, as I've always
> understood—"

The soldiers shrug off the offer. No time for that. Time to burn
this house to the ground. No exceptions. Only there's something
else. Once the sisters and their last loyal servant finally agree to
leave the house (Delilah herself is dragged), it becomes alarm-
ingly clear that someone—a child—is still inside. A little boy

named Phinny who, for unclear reasons, is always kept out of sight upstairs. Nothing to be done. What can it matter now? With everything going to hell like this? If the house must burn, let it burn now.

When it came—but it was a bellowing like a bull, that came from inside—Delilah drew close, with Miss Theo's skirt to peep around, and Miss Theo's face looked down like death itself and said, "Remember this. You black monkeys," as the blaze outdid them all.

In the aftermath, the two sisters and Delilah walk, dazed, through the smoking ruins of Jackson, which, like their house, has also just been torched to the ground. Imagine wandering lost around a city that no longer exists. The three point out landmarks to each other, what had been at this corner, what had been across this street.

"The State House."—"The school."
"The Blind School."—"The penitentiary."
"The big stable."—"The Deaf-and-Dumb."

At this point in the story, though, Myra begins moaning about Phinny, who she now claims was her child. Theo replies, "Don't you know he's black?"

Myra is clearly losing what's left of her mind. But jagged pieces of a family secret begin to fall together. Phinny, it emerges, was fathered by Myra and Theo's brother, Benton, years ago, when he raped another child—Delilah herself. Back then Delilah had named her son Jonah. When they took him away from her (the boy must have been too light-skinned for the slave quarters), they renamed the boy Phinny.

And it was better to let that mixed-race child burn alive than suffer the humiliation of revealing his existence in front of Union soldiers. Myra's response to Theo takes the grotesque scenario to an outer limit, and it's been seared into my memory since the first time I read the story:

"He *was* white." Then, "He's black *now*."

Why didn't Delilah shout bloody murder when they were about to burn the house? Why does she do nothing to save her own child? A reader is left to wonder about Delilah's numbness. There are no heroics in Welty's depiction of enslavement, and there will be no redemption, either. As the three women walk amid the ruins, Delilah suffers the grief that Myra and Theo lack the humanity to face. "The Burning" is an act of exposure. The fact that it retains the power to shock is a testament to its endurance. Any false pretense of humor falls away in the final pages. But even here you might find yourself deceived. Because these two ladies can't even hang themselves without first having to climb up on Delilah's shoulders to reach a high-enough branch.

And the July sun blazes like an unheard scream as Delilah returns to the charred house to search for Jonah's bones.

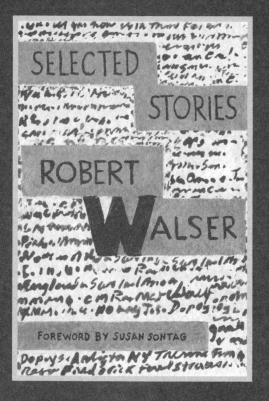

SELECTED

STORIES

ROBERT

WALSER

FOREWORD BY SUSAN SONTAG

WALSER ON MISSION STREET

> How is one to understand an author who was so beset by shadows and who, nonetheless, illumined every page with the most genial light...
>
> —W. G. Sebald

I confess I'm drawn to stories about people who are even more depressed than I am. You, too? Aren't there times when other people's misery has a way of lifting the soul a little? A we're-all-in-this-together sort of thing?

Let's get the man's death out of the way. At his family's urging, the fifty-one-year-old Swiss writer Robert Walser checked himself into a sanitarium for a psychiatric evaluation in 1929. He'd begun to hear voices. The family was afraid that he could no longer take care of himself. He was diagnosed with schizophrenia, although he continued to write. Four years later he was forcibly transferred to an insane asylum. There, it is said, the always prolific writer of often very tiny stories ceased to write altogether. I didn't come here to write, he is said to have told a visiting friend, I came here to be crazy. It is tempting to add something Walser may not have said out loud but may have meant: *You think being crazy doesn't take work?* At the asylum he is known to have scrubbed vegetables, sorted scraps of tinfoil, read, and sometimes, according to another visitor, stood silently in a corner. He remained at the asylum for twenty-three years. He took long walks. One frigid winter day, while roaming in an adjacent forest, Walser had a heart attack. Later, some children found his frozen body in the snow. Police took photographs. Walser's hat lies a few feet from his head. These pictures have been widely reproduced now that Walser has come into some posthumous international fame. *Look at the dead writer.* This is how greatness ends up. Sprawled, alone, forgotten. There are paintings of Walser lying in the snow, always with his hat a few feet from his head. Online I found a clever photographic reenactment. A young woman stretched out in the snow. Again, there's that hat just out of reach. But would the corpse of a seventy-eight-year-old accountant who'd lost his hat have looked any more abandoned lying in the snow?

Before he stopped writing (if he did stop writing, maybe he continued to compose in his head*), Robert Walser wrote some of the most peculiarly wondrous stories of the last century. Among them is "Kleist in Thun," about the German writer Heinrich von Kleist. Kleist was the author of "The Marquise of O," a story that begins with this sentence:

> In M——, an important town in northern Italy, the widowed Marquise of O——, a lady of unblemished reputation and the mother of several well-brought-up children, inserted the following announcement in the newspapers: that she had,

---

*It's also conceivable that at the asylum his work was confiscated and destroyed.

without knowledge of the cause, come to find herself in a certain situation; that she would like the father of the child she was expecting to disclose his identity to her; that she was resolved, out of consideration to her family, to marry him.

A certain situation!

Walser's homage to Kleist, in turn, opens with a far more mundane recounting of facts. A narrator is visiting the town of Thun, and he comes upon a marble plaque on a house identifying it as a place where Kleist once lived for a time. We never learn exactly what the plaque says. Presumably some banter like: *In this house once slept the legendary German writer Heinrich von Kleist, author of* Michael Kohlhaas *and "The Marquise of O" and other world-renowned works.* And yet the idea of Kleist having lived in this very house gets the narrator's imagination going. From the plaque Walser moves, seamlessly, without so much as clearing his throat, directly into Kleist's psyche, as the man himself wanders around Thun taking in the sights—in 1802.

> Spring has come. Around Thun the fields are thick with flowers, fragrance everywhere, hum of bees, work, sounds fall, one idles about; in the heat of the sun you could go mad. It is as if radiant red stupefying waves rise up in his head whenever he sits at his table and tries to write. He curses his craft. He had intended to become a farmer when he came to Switzerland. Nice idea, that. Easy to think up in Potsdam. Poets anyway think up such things easily enough. Often he sits at the window.

I've got a friend, Gabe, who manages her family farm in Brunswick, Georgia. Much succulent produce is grown there. I have always wondered what it would be like to just pick up and leave my life, get on a Greyhound and throw myself into working the fertile Sapelo soil. Harvest the fruit of my own labor. I'd be as useless and daydreamy as Kleist.

Often he sits at the window.

Why does this line strike me as funny? It's hard to say exactly. I relate, that's part of it. If I had a window in this garage, I'd be looking out it right now. I think a lot of people sitting in places without windows spend a lot of their lives looking out windows that don't exist.

Kleist will shoot himself (and his terminally ill girlfriend) a few years after his stay in Thun, a fact that is left out of the story, and yet at the same time is present, at least tonally, in every sentence. Kleist, in Walser's rendering, is becoming unhinged; he lurches from suffering to ecstasy, often in the same paragraph, sometimes within the same sentence. Walser so inhabits his character that from the beginning you forget that there's somebody from another era narrating this story. Kleist overcomes you, so fully are you within his mind and his heart as he tries, vainly, to control the sensations that are flooding his imagination. He's feeling much too much. He can't tamp down his emotional response to everything within his line of sight. Everything—everything—he sees in this perfect little Swiss town begins to take on sacred significance.

> Sundays Kleist likes, and market days also, when everything ripples and swarms with blue smocks and the costumes of the peasant women on the road, and on the narrow main street. . . . Grocers announce their cheap treasures with beguiling country cries. And usually on such a market day there shines the most brilliant, the hottest, the silliest sun. Kleist likes to be pushed hither and thither by the bright bland throng of folk. Everywhere there is the smell of cheese.

All is so radiant you'd think Kleist is actually happy. And he is. He's happy in the way certain depressed people can be sometimes, recklessly happy. It's happened to me more than a few times. When I feel so good my chest starts to hurt and I worry I'm having a heart attack.

> He walks on, past women with skirts lifted high, past girls who carry baskets on their heads, calm, almost noble, like the Italian women carrying jugs he has seen in paintings, past shouting men and drunken men, past policemen, past schoolboys moving with their schoolboy purposes, past shadowy alcoves which smell cool, past ropes, sticks, foodstuffs, imitation jewelry, jaws, noses, hats, horses, veils, blankets, woolen stockings, sausages, balls of butter, and slabs of cheese . . .

Alice Munro once wrote that she was in such awe of Eudora Welty's prose, all she could do in an essay was throw up her hands and quote her. I feel the same way about Walser's sentences. Even in translation, this joyous list floors me. Woolen stockings, sausages, balls of butter, noses. All that cheese. Can't you see it? All the bounty, all the bland Swiss prosperousness? Walser's Kleist is the sort of person who becomes more alive the more he watches other people going about their business. And think about it: if you pause a little and simply watch people, doesn't the world have a way of turning miraculous? This early morning, out for a walk along Mission Street, I stopped in front of Sun Fat Seafood between Twenty-second and Twenty-third and watched the arrival of the day's delivery. Two men were draining fish from a tank attached to the back of a flatbed truck into a large yellow barrel set on the street. Some of the fish didn't make it into the barrel, and I watched one—it looked like a mackerel—flop onto Mission Street.

There was something thrilling about a fish fighting for life in the middle of traffic. Soon a Chevy with shiny chrome hubcaps ended it.

Now, I may have been under the spell of Walser at that moment. I'd been reading "Kleist in Thun" as I was walking down the sidewalk. So it may be that I was especially alive to the details of my own world, details that I often ignore. But in a larger sense I think it was simply because I'd stopped to watch. I'd never thought about it before. How do fish get into the fish store? I know how they get out of the ocean. But the actual store? And there it all was. On Mission Street. A truck, a tank, a barrel. The whole story with the wrong ending. A lone mackerel crushed dead by a souped-up Impala.

Maybe we write in order to try to feel things we know we should feel in life but don't. Maybe we write—and read—because we don't pay enough attention. Yet in Kleist's case, or at least in Walser's imagining of Kleist's case, his attempt to replicate what he saw and felt watching the good people of Thun fails. Kleist recognizes that he isn't up to it. Why write if words are so pale in comparison to what he takes in simply by looking out his window?

He wants to perish into the image. He wants eyes alone, only to be one single eye.

Not that paying intense attention itself is cheap. And maybe this is why we so often do our best to avoid it. I stood there enraptured by a fish dying in the street but after that, my nose in a book, I hardly noticed a woman curled up in a fetal position on the sidewalk on the corner of Mission and Cesar Chavez. Kleist, according to Walser, missed nothing and was, eventually, overcome.

The Burning Plain
and Other Stories

by

Juan Rulfo

Translated by
George Schad

ON THE BEAUTY OF NOT WRITING
or
AN UNNECESSARY HOMAGE TO JUAN RULFO

I would like to be even more silent. Unlike the urge to read, which is an ever-present ache, the urge to write comes only once in a while, and when it does, I do my best to keep it short. The upshot of much advice about writing seems to be: *Write, write a lot. When you are done writing a lot, write some more.* I have some serious doubts about this always being the best route to the creation of something enduring. Am I alone? Or do you find yourself longing to escape from a daily tsunami of words? Recently, I considered writing a homage to a writer who, in his lifetime, published less than three hundred pages. After taking a few notes, I became aware of the obvious contradiction. For a while, I did the right thing. I thought about Juan Rulfo without making sentences. Why add any more words to a legacy built on so few? I'm about to undo that small amount of progress.

Juan Rulfo published two books, a story collection, *The Burning Plain,* in 1953 and a novel, *Pedro Páramo,* two years later. Of *Pedro Páramo*, García Márquez claimed he revered the book so much that once he memorized every word in order to internalize its rhythms. I believe him. For decades, readers in Mexico and around the world waited for another book. They waited, and they waited. Rulfo died in 1986 at the age of sixty-nine. No new work of fiction has ever appeared.

When asked why he stopped writing, Rulfo once told an interviewer that he'd heard most of his stories from a favorite uncle. What happened, Rulfo said, was that this uncle died. Has any writer given a better answer to this presumptuous question? Only someone who's never written fiction would be fool enough to ask it. My view is this: A writer's silence (or anybody's) should never be interrogated, only respected, and this from a distance.

In an introduction to *Pedro Páramo*, Susan Sontag wrote:

> Everyone asked Rulfo why he did not publish another book, as if the point of a writer's life is to go on writing and publishing. In fact, the point of a writer's life is to produce a great book—that is, a book that will last—and this is what Rulfo did. No book is worth reading once if it is not worth reading many times.

I'd like to make an amendment to Sontag's otherwise gracious thought. Rulfo wrote not one but *two* lasting books. I know of no other novel that approaches the nearly overwhelming—call it orchestral—multivoiced, ghostly, time-bending, and doomful intensity of *Pedro Páramo*.

> At daybreak the village was awakened by the ringing of the bells. It was the morning of the eighth of December. A gray morning, but not cold. The ringing began with the largest bell, and the others followed it. A few people thought they were ringing for High Mass, and began to open their doors. But only a few, only those who wake up before dawn and lie awake until the first bells tell them the night has ended. But the ringing went on longer than it should have.

In the novel, the narrator searches for his father, Pedro Páramo, in an underworld that is as hellish and, at times, as tender as our world. And yet I return, again and again, to Rulfo's first book to re-experience something even more fundamental: how to inhabit a story by simply listening.

Because I forget this. I spend so much time alone in my head that I forget what it is like to open myself up to the voice of a stranger. In my aborted notes, I intended to focus on a brief story (all the stories in *The Burning Plain* are under ten pages) called "Luvina." Two men, a drunk and a traveler, are drinking in a bar by the side of a road. Outside, some children are playing by the river. The drunk, in exchange for drinks, is telling the traveler about the town where the traveler is now headed—a place called Luvina. The drunk says that in Luvina the wind blows so hard it "takes the roofs off houses as if they were hats," and the rain falls for only a few days a year. Some years it never falls at all. Luvina, the drunk says, is a desperate place—dry as old leather, too cold in the winter, too hot in the summer—where the only thing one can hope for is the inevitable peace of death itself. The drunk talks on. He's a former schoolteacher who himself once went to Luvina with youthful expectations.

> In those days I was strong. I was full of ideas—you know how we're all full of ideas. And one goes with the idea of making something of them everywhere. But it didn't work out in Luvina. I made the experiment and it failed—

The traveler doesn't say much. We never learn what he thinks about his own journey to Luvina. Is he afraid? Or does he believe that his own youth—I read the traveler as young, though there isn't any direct evidence—will be stronger than the drunk's and that Luvina won't defeat him? At one point, the drunk pauses and is quiet for a while. The narrator, a disembodied voice hovering above the story, breaks in to tell us:

> The flying ants entered and collided with the oil lamp, falling to the ground with scorched wings. And outside night kept on advancing.

What could I possibly say about "Luvina" that isn't encompassed in: *And outside night kept on advancing.* Doesn't it? For us all? Always?

That's as far as I got with my homage.

Right now I am sitting alone at a picnic table in Butano State Park, not far from Pescadero, California. A family of what I've decided must be Russians are sitting a few feet away from me, and I've been listening to them bellow at each other for the past hour. My first thought was they were having an overheated fight and that soon they would start murdering each other with their plastic picnic cutlery (at one point, one of them did reach over the table and bop another one on the head with a large piece of ham), but it's become clear that this is just the way this particular family converses over lunch. There are only five of them, what seems to be a mother and father, around seventy or so, and possibly their three adult children, two men and one woman, all in their late forties, early fifties. There's only five of them, but they make the noise of twenty marauding Cossacks. They are all large people, yet it is their voices that are truly giant. They yowl, they laugh, they bang their mammoth hands on the picnic table. My monolinguality shames me—once again. In my next life, I will learn Russian if it kills me. I'll read

Chekhov and Turgenev and Isaac Babel. I'll drink in Gogol in the original! I'll relocate to Moscow and eavesdrop on an entire country's most intimate conversations.

I've come to this place for the quiet of the redwoods (and something called a fern canyon), and instead I've become mesmerized by the raucous. Forget the flora and the fauna; it's these wild, off-the-rails people I want to be around. I've come for them. And for some reason I'm reminded of Juan Rulfo. What does Rulfo, master of silence, of concision, have to do with the Dostoevskian lunch booming at the next table? Not much, of course, at least on the surface, but as I sit here, the thought lurches into my mind that Rulfo might have enjoyed listening to these people. Maybe his uncle was a boom talker. Is it just me? Or do you, too, sometimes commune with dead writers as with dead friends? Rulfo's just joined me at the table (a gleaming white shirt, a camera slung over his shoulder), though, of course, he's not saying anything. But he's got me thinking of his stories and how they so often revolve around characters telling each other stories. And if I had to guess what my friends at the next table are doing, I'd say they are swapping stories—stories each of them has probably heard hundreds of times already.

I've come to believe: as often as not, it's not the telling, it's the repeating. Rulfo's work at its core is about people unburdening themselves of the stories they can't stop telling. It's for this reason, above all, I think, that Rulfo is here with me at this obscure state park, at this dinky picnic area, listening to a language that he can't understand either. I also believe—and maybe so does Rulfo's shade—that the stories these exuberant picnickers are telling each other, in their own inimitable way, have something to do with what happened to all the aspirations they had when they were younger. Lately, I've begun to feel the faith I used to have in myself slowly ebbing away. At what point in our lives do we fall so in love with our own failures that we can't stop talking about them? At one point do we clam up for good?

As I think of "Luvina" now (again I don't have the book I most need*), I'm the traveler in the bar who thinks, without saying it out loud, that I'm finally going to turn my life around. I'm heading to a place called Luvina, where everything, at last, is going to be different.

> I was a teacher. I'd come there to work at the school. When I arrived there with my family, there was nobody around to greet us. I sent my wife around to look for some food. She was gone for hours. I finally went and searched and found her kneeling alone in an empty church. I asked her what was taking her so long, why didn't she go to find some food? She said, shhhh, she wasn't finished praying. Because she, unlike me, understood where we'd ended up. That night the whole family slept huddled together in the cold church. Just before dawn, I woke up to a strange sound. At first I thought it was bat wings. Still half asleep, I went to the door of the church and saw a group of old women in black dresses rustling slowly by, empty jugs on their shoulders.

A foolish thing to try and channel a hero. If I got it all wrong, if my cadences are all off, if I failed to replicate anything close to a true Rulfoan rhythm, it is because I lack the skill. But I do know at least one thing for certain: The dresses of those old women rustled like bats as they walked by the church just before dawn. Because this detail has been lodged in my memory since I first encountered "Luvina." I remember looking up from the page to try to listen to the way that fabric of those dresses rubbed together to produce that singular sound. His people may not have a lot to say, but this doesn't make them any less vital. How did he do it? He said he

*Sometimes I worry that one day I'll break down and buy an infernal Kindle.

84

listened to his uncle's stories. Okay, but I also think Rulfo listened to the silence that follows us all around like a premature death.

The old drunk drinks and talks a little more. He says in spite of the omens, he stuck it out in Luvina. He'd made a go of it. Years later, after the place had already destroyed him, he finally fled. But by then it was too late. The town of Luvina had already become his story, the one he tells and retells to anyone—you?—who will listen (and buy him a mescal or two), the one about that time when he was young and so full of expectations.

Chekhov wrote: "The Russian loves recalling life, but he does not love living."

This might be true of us all. But recalling *is* living. And our defeats *are* our stories. I've failed here, too. I've gone on too long about the beauty of not writing. This is no homage. But stories have got to be told. I say, tell them, tell them sparingly if you can, but tell them. And when the telling is done, like my California Russians who have now retreated, utterly spent, to sagging lawn chairs, like the old drunk teacher who rests his worn-out head on the bar, it will be time to sleep.

2

LET ME
COOK YOU
AN EGG

To tell the truth, there's no more or less wind here than anywhere else, no more or less love here than anywhere else, no
more or less lowdown dishonesty than anywhere else.

—Lyonel Trouillot, *Street of Lost Footsteps*

Penguin Modern Classics

Virginia Woolf

To the Lighthouse

UPPER MOOSE LAKE, 1990

I'm twenty-two, I'm drunk, I'm in a canoe. The Boundary Waters of northern Minnesota: Midwestern heaven, mosquitoes the size of St. Bernards be damned. It was up north—on Upper Moose Lake— that I found myself transfixed by another watery place. A blazing day, upper 80s, and I was base-camping with two old friends. Boundary Waters trips were always an excuse to base-camp, another term for just sitting around all day and bullshitting. What happened to sitting around all day and bullshitting? Goshko and Alex were in a canoe on one side of the lake, fishing and drinking. I was on the other side, in another boat, reading and drinking. I'd propped myself up on the stern, a life jacket as my pillow. With both hands I held a book up against the sun and tried not to finish it.

There are certain rare books. You know the ones I'm talking about. Finishing is agony because you know you will never again read *this book* for the first time.

Lily Briscoe is painting a picture, or at least she's trying to. Things are going badly and Lily's frustrated. Bizarre to me now that reading about someone not painting well could be so spellbinding.

And I remember lying in the stern of that canoe and slowing down, almost to a standstill, the water lapping the boat, and counting the pages I had left—the paragraphs, the sentences, the words, the letters—when a dragonfly ambushed me and drilled so deep into my left eye socket it was like somebody twisting a screwdriver into my face. I screamed and fell out of the boat. When I broke the surface of the frigid lake, I could hear Goshko and Alex yawning across the water. *Orner fell in the lake again.* But all that mattered was Lily Briscoe. She was floating, calmly, a few feet away. I let the canoe drift, rescued the book, and swam it to shore. I laid that waterlogged novel on a rock in the sun. And I waited. I sat down beside the rock, watched my canoe wander around the lake by itself, and waited for the book to dry so I could turn the pages again without their sticking together.

I'm not an especially patient person, and in my twenties I was less so, and yet I didn't do anything else. I just waited. True, I'd been drinking, and I've always been convinced that I concentrate better after a few beers. In the Boundary Waters we start drinking in the morning while still in our sleeping bags. But I know that something else beyond five or six Leinenkugels had taken hold of me. It took me at least an hour before I could start reading again, and even then the words bled through the wet pages.

I reread *To the Lighthouse* this week. I wondered about my younger self. Who was this guy so entranced by a book that I'd sit and wait for it to dry? It couldn't have been the plot. For me, it usually isn't. Plot is what goes on in the rest of the world while I'm trying to remember how the light looked under the door from the hall when I was a kid and couldn't sleep. Plot is the low noise of my parents' voices as they argue deep into the night. My mother tries in vain to keep my father quiet. That bar of light, my mother's too loud whispering. My father erupting into a hiss. *Let them hear us, let every nosy piece of shit in this entire town hear us.* In the dark I count the sea horses prancing up and down the wallpaper.

And in fact, in Part III, "The Lighthouse," the final section that had me so entranced, nothing much happens at all, aside from Lily having trouble with her painting. We lose Mrs. Ramsay, the beating heart of the novel, in Part II. She actually dies, if you remember, in brackets.

> [Mr Ramsay, stumbling along a passage one dark morning, stretched his arms out, but Mrs Ramsay having died rather suddenly the night before, his arms, though stretched out, remained empty.]

This has to be the saddest afterthought in fiction. By the end of the novel, all the characters—and all the book's readers—can't stop reaching in the dark for Mrs. Ramsay. Mrs. Ramsay is gone, all seek Mrs. Ramsay. The final section focuses on people who have returned to the scene of what they believe was their greatest happiness, the times they spent at the Ramsays' summer house off the coast of Scotland, before the war. They can't let go of that past, of their memories of Mrs. Ramsay, who was—and this might be the most holy thing about the whole book—a beautifully ordinary person. She was a loving mother who tried to do right by her kids, a wife who doted on her husband even though he didn't always deserve it, a host who liked to bring people together. She was also someone who could be seductively aloof.

Mrs. Ramsay could be my sanctified mother. She could be yours.

Lily Briscoe tries, through painting, to replicate the old feeling of being back at the summer house. She can't do it. She can't translate her visions to the canvas. And can't I relate? How many hours a day do I now spend trying to trap my own ghosts? Words, like paint, will always be static, while the life we work so hard to animate remains forever in motion. Mrs. Ramsay, even in death, is so dynamic in Lily's mind, yet a single person's unknowables are infinite.

> One wanted fifty pairs of eyes to see with, she reflected. Fifty pairs of eyes were not enough to get round that one woman with, she thought. Among them must be one that was stone blind to her beauty. One wanted most some secret sense, fine as air, with which to steal through keyholes and surround her where she sat knitting, talking, sitting silent in the window alone; which took to itself and treasured up, like the air which held the smoke of the steamer, her thoughts, her imaginations, her desires. What did the hedge mean to her, what did the garden mean to her, what did it mean to her when a wave broke?

Mercifully, *To the Lighthouse* embraces the creation of the work itself, whether it is bad, good, or indifferent, as the only possible way forward. One pair of eyes is all we've got. The conclusion of *To the Lighthouse* is as generous as it is moving. Lily accepts the fact that her mediocre paintings are going to end up either rolled up under someone's bed or in an attic somewhere or, more likely, thrown out with the trash. Even so, she'll paint. She'll paint. What choice has she got but to paint? The only way to honor her visions of Mrs. Ramsay and those lost days is to try to get them down. Come what may. The failure to capture the vision *is* the vision.

* * *

And what about my drunken younger self, desperate for a book not to end? What about me out there on that rock? Thoughts about the nature of art couldn't have had me so mesmerized. I was twenty-two and all hormones. Was I hot for Lily Briscoe? For sure I was. She wasn't the first literary figure I'd been aroused by (Laura Ingalls Wilder), nor will she be the last. And Lily wasn't taken, either. She and Charles Tansley never did get together as Mrs. Ramsay had once schemed, so long ago.

Rereading the book, I stood in solemn awe of its indelibility. I was duly astonished by the technical risks that Woolf takes on page after page. It's like watching aerial acrobatics. And I was emotionally wrecked, too. While Mr. Carmichael lies in bed reading Virgil, the Ramsays drop like flies. First Mrs. Ramsay, then Prue just after giving birth, then Andrew is blown up in France during the war . . . But I couldn't muster the idiot love I had back then on my rock. What did I know? More than I know now, I think. I was a better reader. I knew how to just exist, without any writerly la-de-da crap, deep inside a book. And I believe what I wanted, even then, along with getting into Lily Briscoe's pants, was to hold on to what the book tries so hard to bring back: irretrievable time. This is what the book does like few others. It regains the weight of what's vanished. How else to say it? Mine was the only wasted youth I'll ever have to waste. Goshko and Alex and I talk, every year we talk, about going back to Upper Moose Lake. We haven't made it back there together in almost a quarter century now. No tragedy, just something that's never happened. Still, can't I grieve for what's been lost, however small it seems? Once, in late summer, I sat drunk on a rock and waited for a book to dry. Two old friends, their quiet murmurs, reached me across the water.

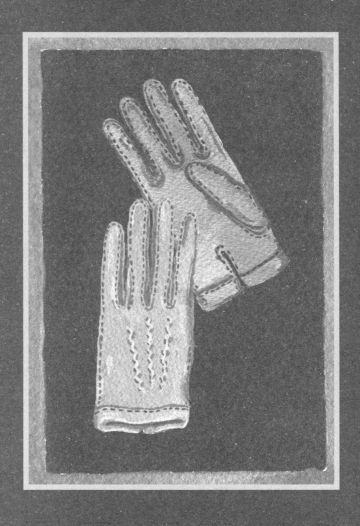

MY FATHER'S GLOVES

I've been trying to lie about this for years. As a fiction writer I feel an almost righteous obligation to the untruth. Yet in many attempts over the years I've not been able to make out of this tiny but sadly soul-defining episode in my life anything more than a plain recounting of facts. Dressing them up into fiction, into a story, wrecked what is essentially a long overdue confession.

I watched my father in the front hall putting on his new lambskin leather gloves. It was like a private ceremony. This was in Chicago, early November 1982. My father had just returned from a business trip to Paris. He'd bought the gloves at a place called Hermès, a mythical wonderland of a department store. He presented the white box to us. He opened it slowly and laid each one on his forearm. He said, Did you know another word for a glove is a gauntlet? Medieval knights were required to wear them. Then he put the gloves on, gingerly, one finger at a time, and held them up to the front hall mirror to see how his own hands looked in such exquisite gauntlets.

A week later, I was home from school. Nobody else was around. I opened the right-hand drawer of the front hall table and there were the Hermès gloves comfortably nested. I learned for the first time how easy it is to just grab something. I stuffed the gloves in my pants and sprinted upstairs to my room. I hid them in the back of my closet under the wicker basket that held my license plate collection. Then I braced myself, for days.

It was a rare warm November.

When we finally left that house on Hazel Avenue—my mother, brother, and I—I took the gloves with me to our new place. I took them with me to college. After I graduated, I took them to Namibia. On a farm outside Karibib, on the edge of the Namib Desert, the oldest desert in the world, it was often cold enough at night for gloves. The wind would suck the 90-degree days right out of the sand. But I never put them on. I still have the gloves, thirty-five-some-odd years later. I've never worn them, not once, although my father and I have the same small hands.

Now that he is older and far milder, it is hard to believe how scared of him I used to be. Back then he was so full of anger. Was he unhappy in his marriage? No doubt. He and my mother never had much in common. She was outgoing and liked people. He liked to hole up at home and hate all the people she wanted to see. But his anger—often it was rage—went beyond this not so unusual mismatch. My own armchair diagnosis is that, as with other chronically unsatisfied people, the daily business of living caused my father despair. At no time did this dissatisfaction manifest itself more powerfully than when he came home from work. A rug askew, a jacket not hung up, a window left open, a water glass in the sink—all could set off a fury. My brother once spilled a pot of ink on the snowy white carpet of my parents' bedroom: Armageddon.

Yet his unpredictability is what made his explosions so potent. Sometimes the bomb wouldn't go off and he'd act, somewhat, like our idea of a normal dad. In December, when he finally noticed that his precious Hermès gloves were missing, my father seemed only confused.

"Maybe they're in the glove compartment," my mother said.

"Impossible," my father said. "The glove compartment is for maps."

"Oh well." My mother shrugged. "You can go to Fell's and get a new pair—"

"Fell's? Red Fell doesn't know gloves from galoshes."

He kept searching the front hall table, as if he had somehow overlooked them amid all the cheap imitation leather gloves, mismatched mittens, and tasseled Chicago Bears hats. I am certain the notion that one of us had taken the gloves never once crossed his mind.

Burdened by guilt (but never enough to return them), I've tried to contort this story into fiction. In my failed attempts, the thief/son *is* always trying to give the gloves back. In one version, the son mails the gloves back to the father, along with a forged letter, purportedly written by a long-dead friend of the father, a man the father had once betrayed. The whole thing was convoluted, but I liked the idea of a package arriving, out of the blue, from an aggrieved ghost. *I'm returning the gloves I stole, Ron. Now at least one of us may be absolved.*

The problem was that this palmed off responsibility on a third party. And it muddied the story by pulling the son/thief out of the center of what little action there was.

In an equally pathetic version, the son (whom I named Jean-Luc for a Parisian touch), home for Thanksgiving, slips the gloves back in the top right-hand drawer of the front hall table of the house he grew up in, the house where the father still lives. This one was marred not only by cooked-up dialogue but also by a dead end.

"Father, you want to take a walk by Lake Michigan?"

"It's been years, Jean-Luc, since we've taken a walk by the lake."

"A chill wind blows. Perhaps you need gloves?"

The moment arrives: the father slides open the right-hand drawer of the front hall table. *Voilà!* Cut to the father's face. Describe his bewilderment. *Qu'est-ce que c'est?* Decades drop from the father's eyes, and both father and son face each other as they never faced each other when both were years younger. The son stammers out a confession. He tries to explain himself, but can't. Why did he take the gloves? Why? And so the story kept collapsing.

It may be that this is a rare case where the truth, whatever this actually is, derails the fiction. I can't give the gloves back, in a story or in this thing we call reality. If I did, I'd have to confront something I've known all along but could never express, even to myself. My father would have given me the damn gloves. All I had to do was ask. He would have been so pleased that for once I liked something he liked. This happened so few times in our lives. All the years I've been trying to write this, maybe I've always known that this fact would stick me in whatever heart I've got left.

Our imaginations sometimes fail us for a reason. Not because it is cathartic to tell the truth, but because coming clean may be a better, if smaller, story. A scared and angry and bewildered kid takes his father's gloves, and ends up carrying them around with him from place to place, rented apartment to rented apartment. Sometimes he takes them out and feels them, but he never puts them on. When I see my father these days, we graze each other's cheeks, a form of kissing in my family. I love my father. I suppose I did then, even in the worst moments of fear.

Well-made things eventually deteriorate. The Hermès gloves are no longer baby-soft. All the handless years have dried them up. I never wanted the gloves. I only wanted you not to have them. In 1982, you weren't much older than I am at this moment, Dad. I think of you now, standing in the front hall, holding your gloves up to the mirror, a rare stillness on your face, a kind of hopeful calm. Was this what I wanted to rip right off your hands?

WILLIAM MAXWELL

All the DAYS and NIGHTS

THE COLLECTED STORIES

UNFORGIVABLE

This morning I threw a novel out the window of my car. This occurred at approximately 11:30 a.m. at the corner of Westlake and Miriam Street in Daly City, California. It was raining. I was on my way to the Red Wing store in the Westgate Shopping Center. I needed new bootlaces. I was reading a few lines from a novel— Julian Barnes's *The Sense of an Ending*—at a red light. I often keep a book under the seat for long lights. After a few paragraphs (I'm a turtle of a slow reader, but you should wait at a red light in Daly City), I found myself, once again, sympathizing with Adrian, a character who, before the book opens, kills himself to get away from people like Tony, the guy telling us the story. I believe Tony is supposed to be a charmingly irritating fellow. All I got was irritated. I'm sure I'm unfair. Smarter heads than mine, people I love and respect, adored this novel, including my mother. It was her book-club copy that I lobbed into the street.

Still, what happened happened. Too late for me to take it back. The sentence that sent me over was something along the lines of

"I wrote an e-mail to Veronica and wrote in the subject line: *Question: Do you think I was in love with you back then?*"

Leaving aside that I read to get away from e-mail, I'd begun to sense that there was something too cooked up, not only about the e-mail itself, but also about the mystery at the center of the book, something too transparently dishonest about the withholding nature of Tony's guilt. I could feel him treading water before the revelation of something that would be sure to astonish book clubs. I couldn't take it anymore. So, uncharacteristic for the book hoarder I am, I unloaded it. As I drove through the intersection, in the rearview I watched a woman stop in the middle of the cross-walk and examine the discarded book. She was carrying a shopping bag in one hand and an umbrella in the other. This woman deftly and, I thought, with a great deal of style swung the umbrella up, lodged the shaft under her armpit so that the canopy bloomed out behind her, swooped her free hand low, and seized the book. Then she shoved it into one of the big pockets of her raincoat.

When I returned home with my new laces, I found myself freed up once again to choose a new book out of the infinite dark that constitutes all the unread books in the universe. I'm daunted by the possibilities. Maybe this time I will find the one book that will save me from myself. Sometimes, as a kind of temporary solace, and also to stave off the commitment issues I have with new books, I go for something I've already read and loved before I resume the search for *the one book that will save me from myself.* Today, I reached for William Maxwell, a man who, I'd argue, never published a dishonest sentence in his life.

It is raining even harder now. It has been at it for four or five or six days straight. I'm losing track. There's a leak in our bathroom, a rhythmic crashing that provides a kind of beat to my reading. Let it rain. I pray that the sun never rises again over Bernal Hill. Bring on the deluge. Today I'm reading William Maxwell.

* * *

"With Reference to an Incident at a Bridge" is such a brief story that some might relegate it to the status of anecdote. Or worse, a vignette, whatever this even is. "Incident at a Bridge" has little action, little character development; it's just a voice, really. Not all that different, in a way, from *The Sense of an Ending*, which also relies heavily on the voice of one character. Except: William Maxwell does not tread water. His sentences are as clear, and as potentially deadly, as water itself.

We're in the small town of Lincoln, Illinois, early in the last century. The narrator is a twelve-year-old Boy Scout. Like Tony, this Boy Scout, too, is a little irritating. He's a Goody Two-shoes who, in his own words, "went out of my way to help elderly people across the street who could have managed perfectly well on their own." This kid and a few of his fellow Boy Scouts organize a group of younger boys into a troop of Cub Scouts, ostensibly to teach them the ropes.

> We taught the Cub Scouts how to tie a clove hitch and a running bowline and how (if you were lucky) to build a fire without any matches and other skills appropriate to the outdoor life. Somebody, after a few weeks, decided that there ought to be an initiation. Into what I don't think we bothered to figure out.

This power to haze, to initiate—as it so often does—goes to the heads of the older boys. In "Incident at a Bridge" the narrator and his fellow Scouts blindfold the recruits, among them a kid named Maxie Rabinowitz (the son of a broke Jewish shopkeeper from the wrong side of town), and march them to the outskirts of town. They stop at a bridge. The narrator then orders these small blindfolded boys to run straight ahead as fast as they can. The boys do as they are told, and one by one they each slam directly into the railing at the side of the bridge. The impact knocks the wind out of every one of them. None of the boys is seriously injured, but the incident haunts the narrator, an inexplicable act of violence perpetrated for no reason.

Some readers conflate the deceptively genial first-person narrator William Maxwell employs in many of his stories and novels with Maxwell himself. I've heard it said, and by people who should know better, that Maxwell mostly wrote nonfiction. As if the trick to his method was merely a transcription of real events. Maxwell himself may have encouraged this sort of interpretation when he said in an interview that he never made much up, that he wasn't that sort of writer. But certain rare fiction writers contort their own memories into something greater: myth. And so, here, a moment on a bridge in a small Illinois town in the 1920s becomes immortalized, burned into the souls of anybody who reads about it.

We have all done things we wish we could erase, forever, from the record. No matter how we airbrush our own histories, the hurt we have caused will, always, reach out for us—like for me today— out of the December rain. Among the many, many worse things I've done is something that might seem, like Maxwell's transgression, minor in the course of a long life. In the seventh grade, I used to sing a song to a fat kid named Theodore. It went to the tune of Foreigner's "Hot Blooded." The chorus went like this:

> *Big-butted, check it and see*
> *All you gotta do is look behind Teddy*

Every day for a year, during gym class, I sang that fucking song. And God knows, like I say, I've done a lot worse, and a lot more recently. This is the only thing, on a long list of things, I'd take back. This is why Maxwell's story transcends anecdote. Because the story refuses any absolution. You live with it, period.

> I believe in the forgiveness of sins. Some sins. I also believe that what is done is done and cannot be undone. The reason I didn't throw myself on my knees in the dust and beg them (and God) to forgive me is that I knew He wouldn't, and that even if He did, I wouldn't forgive myself. Sick with shame at the pain I had inflicted, I tore Max Rabinowitz's blindfold off and held him by the shoulders until his gasping subsided.

There is something frighteningly counterintuitive about the narrator's inability to forgive himself. *God might have mercy on me, but I never will.*

Although the narrator of "Incident at a Bridge" is Presbyterian, and he recites the Apostle's Creed on the opening page, *I believe in the Holy Ghost, the holy catholic church, the communion of saints, the forgiveness of sins,* the story reminds me of something my old rabbi in Chicago once said on Yom Kippur. Rabbi Marx, who was later run out of our congregation for marrying a non-Jewish woman (another story, but one that should, to this day, bring shame to those who ran him off for loving somebody), once said something I have never forgotten: *You want atonement? For that you must go and ask the forgiveness of those you've sinned against. Start tonight.*

In other words, you can't just go straight to God. My gut sinks to remember those words, at the work I have to do, at the work that is probably too late to do. I could start with Teddy and work my way forward. But I've got a class to teach. And I've got to pick up my kid at day care at 4:30. And what about all the people I'll hurt tomorrow? You're talking about a full-time forgiveness operation here. Who's got time?

What "Incident at a Bridge" does, finally, is instruct the narrator on the nature of his own heart. Here's the final resplendent paragraph in full.

> Considering the multitude of things that happen in any one person's life, it seems fairly unlikely that those little boys remembered the incident for very long. It was an introduction to what was to come. And cruelty could never again take them totally by surprise. But I have remembered it. I have remembered it because it was the moment I learned I was not to be trusted.

. . .

KADDISH FOR A CHILD NOT BORN

IMRE KERTESZ

WHILE READING IMRE KERTÉSZ

Half-asleep on a bench in the park near the Cesar Chavez exit off the 101, pleasantly drugged by the gentle waft of exhaust fumes drifting from the crawling traffic, the sun hot on my face, the pigeons serenely hunting the asphalt beneath me, a few dogs barking, the whap and roll of the skateboards—I think of the skateboarders, their intense, silent concentration, if I could concentrate on a sentence, Jesus, If I could concentrate on anything, the way they do on the curve of a ramp—when a voice, feminine in nature, speaks:

"What book are you reading that makes you fall asleep?"

I squint into the light. In the sun's glare all I can see are the top of what are apparently bright yellow jeans. Exposed flesh. A belly button. I imagine this voice emanating from said belly button, which when you think about it is kind of like a little mouth. Still, I am always a little put off when people ask me what book I'm reading. I find it the kind of aggressive act whose intent, it seems, is to make me stop reading because something about it is making the questioner uncomfortable. Why does reading freak so many people out? Normally I flash the offender an unfamiliar title emblazoned with, if I'm lucky, an unpronounceable foreign name. That usually scares off more conversation. Even though I have such a book in this instance, there is something about her voice. I say, "A novel by Imre Kertész. And I'm not sleeping, I'm dozing." I still can't see her. I'm still lying down and the sun is still blazing white in my eyes. "Hungarian. Writes about the Holocaust."

"Oh," the belly button voice says, and sits down beside my feet on what little room is left on the bench. "Recreational reading."

"There's no such thing as recreational reading."

"Oh."

She doesn't say "Oh" as in sounds interesting, maybe I'll check that out sometime. It's an open-ended Oh, a keep-talking sort of Oh, but only if I want to. Within that Oh, silence is okay by her, too. Holocaust literature as pickup line. This is low-rent Woody Allen. For a while I don't say anything, I just keep lying there, squinting, gripping the book to my chest.

"It's about a guy who survives—he's actually born at Auschwitz— but later in life he kills himself. Before that, his wife leaves him because he refuses to have children. Because how do you bring up a child in a world like this? You know what I mean? How could anyone blame him? To this guy bringing a child into a world where such nightmares become real amounts to almost a sadistic thing to do. At the very least, selfish. So the only honorable course of action, the only holy decision he can make, is to repudiate his own flesh. Okay, not the happiest of books. And it's pretty much all one conversation this guy's having with himself, one long, demented but at the same time completely rational conversation he's having with himself, based on a conversation he once had with this other guy, Dr. Oblath, who may or may not exist. It's a mesmerizing book, actually. Utterly and completely—"

"Except that you fell asleep."

"Well, sometimes the sentences go on for days, but it's brilliant, every sorrowful word is—"

"Uh-huh."

"There's a lull in the middle."

"Oh."

"While he lives his life. After Auschwitz."

"Right."

"Could happen to anybody. You don't need to have lived through—"

"Uh-huh."

"Kaddish means a mourner's prayer. In this case, a Kaddish for a child that was never even conceived. A child who was only an idea, that never breathed a single breath and yet he prays and he prays—"

"I know what Kaddish means," says the voice.

After a few minutes of silence she squeezes my right foot, not hard, just saying hello and so long in a single gesture. She's gone. I go back to reading. *"No!" something within me bellowed, howled, instantly and at once, and my whimpering abated only gradually, after the passage of long years, into a sort of quiet but obsessive pain until, slowly and malignantly, like an insidious illness, a question assumed ever more definite form within me: Would you be a brown-eyed little girl, with the pale specks of your freckles scattered around your tiny nose? Or else a headstrong boy, your eyes bright and hard as greyish-blue pebbles?*

What Was Lost
Herbert Morris

Poems

UNDER ALL THIS NOISE

I made the mistake of admitting to a friend that I fantasized about becoming a reclusive writer. Tame, I know, given that the whole point of having a fantasy in the first place is to go whole hog. That's the best you can do? Yet isn't there something seductive about these mysterious figures who squirrel away? We imagine them toiling in a remote mountain cabin or a Manhattan apartment (wife, a publicist) and only rarely and, with much fanfare, releasing book-length dispatches through an intricate web of agents and lawyers, communiqués that allow an anxiously waiting reading public to make sense of the chaos that has become our world. A guru who bursts forth every thirteen or seventeen years like a cicada with the insight to help us carry forward this failed experiment we call civilization.

"Hermit," Thoreau once wrote. "I wonder what the world is doing now."

My friend cut to the chase. "You're not famous enough to be reclusive," he said. "What's the opposite of famous? Everybody else? Maybe you'll get some traction after you're dead."

On the unlikely chance my friend's assessment is doubted, here's an illustration of my relationship to my readers in the form of a recent letter.

Attention Peter Orner:

I introduced myself to you at last year's Jewish Book Festival in San Francisco. There were only two other people present, and one was the lady introducing you, so you might remember me. I'm an Orner too, but we decided we aren't related. In the past 8 months, or more, I have been plagued by calls from T-Mobile. No matter how many times I have sworn to them that no one by the name of Peter Orner lives at this number, they keep calling. They assured me I was being deleted on their computer, but they still call. Please be good enough to call me between 7:30 a.m. and 9:45 a.m., or 7:30 p.m. and 11 p.m., Monday through Thursday, to resolve this matter. Thank you.

Ms. Dvora Orner

My friend might also be right that a person requires a degree of notoriety in order to be known for having disappeared in the first place. And to my discredit, deep down, I admit this is the really attractive part of the whole deal. Yeah, I want to retreat from the world and ponder in solitude. At the same time I wouldn't mind at least a couple of people pondering my whereabouts.

Orner? Didn't he punt for the Vikings?

No, some writer. Went missing before anybody even knew who the hell he was.

But what'd he do before that?

Wrote a few books, but I think he just wanted the fact that he disappeared itself to mean something, you know, in itself.

You sure he wasn't a punter?

I wonder if this yearning to vanish is rooted in my uneasy relationship with how theoretically connected we all are with one another now. Not long ago I attended another literary festival (so much for being reclusive) and I happened to wander into a panel discussion called The Future of the Book as the Book. The prognosis for the book as the book, I learned, is inconclusive. A few actual physical books might be published in the future (as boutique-type items), but then again, they might not. It really depends. On what? Well, on certain variables. Like whether or not there are any physical bookstores or publishers left in the next few decades. Only one thing didn't seem in doubt at all, and that is the future of the *physical* writer of these inconclusive books. A writer's future, we were told, is directly tied to the successful deployment of a "vigorous online persona." A writer, one panelist declared, who doesn't *personally* reach out to readers via social media is DOA. End of story. Nothing to discuss.

This was alarming for several reasons. One is that I've tried social media. I'm never quite sure what to say. I've shared things my friends are doing. I reposted Brad Finkel's picture with the caption *Just back from trip of a lifetime to Banff!!!* This posting netted me: 14 likes. Is this because fourteen people approved of Brad's trip to Banff, or his picture, or the number of exclamation points, or what? Or were they just, you know, supporting my support of Brad's trip of a lifetime? This is confusing. I'm dating myself by the minute here. In any case, the point is I've also posted a few personal things, and some things about what I'm up to so-called professionally, in the overly optimistic belief that such posting might lead to an extra book sale or two. My sales numbers, I've been told, are on life support. *Calling all Kansans, I'll be appearing at the Barnes and Noble in Wichita tonight at 7 p.m. Love to see you all out there. Bring friends,*

uncles, aunts, parolees . . . But each time I've done so, I've been overcome by a dread. The impulse—now an industry, now a much-
studied phenomenon—to spread any and all news about oneself far
and wide has become soul-crushing. It makes me want to retreat to
my garage with my (possibly, it depends on certain variables) out-
moded physical books and unfinished, handwritten manuscripts.
But maybe the fact is, I'm just not all that good at being myself. I've
come to see what people call social media (meaning what exactly?)
is a skill like anything else. Some are talented at it; others less so. I'm
a mediocre interior decorator also. Nor can I cook, play the piano,
speak Italian, change the oil, dance, iron a shirt, or tell a reason-
ably funny joke. Also, and friends will attest to this, I never seem to
understand any jokes anybody else tells, either.

And yet if I don't communicate personally with readers, I'm
DOA? End of story?

There is, though, a more significant issue at stake. The whole point
of fiction has always been to forget about me. God only knows this
is hard enough. But to paraphrase Welty, fiction is the grand art
of seeing the world through another person's eyes. There is something about the demand that fiction writers speak as themselves,
outside their books, that feels like a violation of what Welty held so
sacred. Inventing characters, nonexistent people, and introducing
them into an already overcrowded, indifferent world is an act of
faith, one of the few acts of faith I've got left.

Obviously, social media itself isn't the trouble. Paleolithic man
yowled after a victorious hunt so that other less lucky Paleolithic men would know of his good fortune finding meat. He also
wanted to let his family, friends, colleagues, distant acquaintances,

enemies, and people he'd never met and never would meet, know he was still gluten-free and feeling terrific!!!

The crux, at least as I see it, is that the substance of what we create is, lately, too often considered almost incidental to the way we market our book/product and ourselves/product. Some might argue it's always been thus. To a certain extent, maybe, but I found it telling that during the panel discussion on the future of the book as a book, for instance, what goes inside the books under discussion received passing, almost grudging mention. Just yesterday I read a piece about pricing in self-published e-books. Apparently $3.99 is the sweet spot. Sweet spot? Am I a brontosaurus to wonder what this $3.99 book is actually about?

It may be sharing too much to admit that I take my life cues not only from Eudora Welty but also from the movie *Say Anything*. I'm a child of the '80s. We didn't have that much to guide us. But remember Lloyd Dobler? *I don't want to sell anything, buy anything, or process anything as a career. I don't want to sell anything bought or processed, or buy anything sold or processed, or process anything sold, bought, or processed, or repair anything sold, bought, or processed. You know, as a career, I don't want to do that.*

I've always taken solace in the example of writers who, in spite of all the counterpressures, let their words do all the talking. On my desk, at this moment, sits a book of poetry by someone named Herbert Morris. I've been reading this book for years, and I know zero about Herbert Morris's life. The poet clearly wanted it this way. On the jacket of *What Was Lost*, published in 2000, there is no biographical information. There is no author photo and no information about where the poet lives. There are no acknowledgments. Only the poems. But they are all I've ever wanted and what I especially need right now. I'm in one of my moods. Stymied by my own inadequacies, I want to descend into someone else's life and stay there.

Herbert Morris writes of people, sometimes well-known people such as Henry James (as he sits in a carriage fantasizing about a young doctor) and James Joyce (as he sits on a beach) in moments of profound isolation. One poem, "History, Weather, Loss, the Children, Georgia," is about a photograph taken of Franklin and Eleanor Roosevelt as they sit in their car in front of a group of schoolkids. The photo was taken seconds before the children began a serenade. The poem begins gradually, as Morris constructs the scene in the minutest of detail. The children have been rehearsing all week for this occasion. Their mouths are poised, frozen forever in little Os. Even the threads of their clothes receive attention. As does the hand-printed banner *Welcome Mister President*. Only toward the very last lines does Morris move in on Franklin and Eleanor themselves. These two icons may be long dead, and this haunted moment in Warm Springs, Georgia, in 1938 is long past, but this poem throbs with life. Franklin and Eleanor are not historical props but, rather, two vulnerable human beings sitting together—apart—in the back of an open car. The poet delicately, yet vehemently, chastises Franklin for "his wholly crucial failure" to do something as simple as touch his wife in public.

> or once, once, whisper to her
> intimacies any man might well whisper
> on the brink of the heartbreak of the Thirties
> (the voiceless poised to sing, air strangled, sultry,
> the music teacher's cue not yet quite given . . .)

I can't help but imagine Herbert Morris, whoever he was, staring at this photograph so long and with such absorption that Franklin and Eleanor begin to sweat in the humid air. And still

Franklin's fingers don't reach for Eleanor's. The poem is an elegy for this touch that never happened.

As a reader, this is what I crave. I want flawed characters on the page, people who make colossal mistakes. Human beings. Morris gives us the miracle of other people in their most intimate, unguarded moments. Now more than ever, I want to know about private tribulations, not public achievements. Herbert Morris may not have trumpeted himself when he was alive. He kept himself apart, and the details of his own life were forever left out of the equation. Perhaps as a consequence, he may not have sold many books or reached many readers, but somehow he found his way to me. Books pursue us. I've always believed this. It may take years, decades, a century. I dug Herbert Morris out of the free bin outside Dog Eared Books on Valencia Street in San Francisco. What compelled me to stop that day? How can I express my gratitude to a poet who never sought it, who only wanted me to know his creations, not their creator? And how many others might be out there, somewhere, under all this noise, telling us things we need to hear?

WILLIAM TREVOR

CHEATING AT CANASTA

HIT AND RUN

I'm driving along a dark road, tall pines on both sides. It may be the northern Wisconsin of my twenties. I recognize the road itself. The pavement is reddish. Up there in the far North Woods, in Douglas County, just south of Lake Superior, the roads are tinged red because red local clay was used to build them. Up there are more small lakes than people, and I imagine that the little girl in the white dress had just come from swimming in some murky backwoods pond when she ran into County Road F and into my headlights. I've got no time to swerve. There's a not-very-loud thump. In the rearview, in the dim gloom of the brake lights, I see a white dress sprawled on the pavement. I keep driving into the dark. I've got to get to the Longbranch in Minong to meet friends. The Longbranch in Minong where the giant moose lords over the pool table and the Birch Trail girls in their dark sunglasses and cut-off shorts stand around dangling longnecks from their fingers.

* * *

The North Woods, I dream of them often, and I just figured the girl in white was a fragment of something that could have happened but didn't. Wouldn't I know if it happened? This went on for years. Months would go by and I wouldn't think of it, and then I'd be at a stop sign, say at Twenty-fifth and Capp, and there would be that little girl in the white dress crossing in front of the hood of the car, and I'd know that it happened again the night before. And then, all the rest of that day and into the night, it would gnaw at me. What if sometime, back in the late '80s, I actually hit a little girl and kept driving? Maybe I was drunk and simply blocked the whole thing out. Once, in the night, on my way to drool over the Birch Trail girls, I didn't stop. I never told anybody. I kept this to myself. It didn't happen. It couldn't have happened. But I couldn't stop thinking, What if it happened?

About a week ago now, while reading a story by William Trevor, I began to have an overpowering and sickly feeling of recognition. My vision, dream, whatever it was, was right there on the page. I must have read "The Dressmaker's Child" in 2007, when the book *Cheating at Canasta* first came out, or maybe even earlier in *The New Yorker*. You'd think knowing the source of my nightmare, confirming that it's only a short story (only a short story?) that leaked into my sleep over the years, would bring some relief. It hasn't. The fact that it's a piece of fiction hasn't absolved me of a hit-and-run I didn't commit in Douglas County, Wisconsin, in the late 1980s.

I dreamed it again last night.

It is just after 5:30 in the morning, a cold May dawn in Bolinas. The fog is so thick you can't see the fire station from the corner of Mesa and Overlook, and I walk into the wet miasma by the sewer ponds, thinking, as I often do, about what it would be like to disappear into these vapors for good. I stand and watch the fire station emerge like some church out of a cloudy dream. The dog nudges my leg. Let's get this show on the road. Now I've come back to this kitchen table to scrawl out a few words before I try and go back to sleep. The sun is finally beginning to crawl over Sally's barn, a swash of blood orange beyond the eucalyptus trees. The donkey, Sweet Pea, is groaning her death groans while Fellah stands in his stall with his back to the new day. The dog's already snoozing, but I can't fall back asleep. A dark moth, the kind I was once told is called a Carolina sphinx, a stowaway from last night, just fluttered by my face.

William Trevor leaks into a reader's subconscious. "The Dressmaker's Child" itself, you may not be surprised to hear, like my dream, has a not so latent sexual element. In my version, I'm driving alone to see the Birch Trail girls in their cutoffs. In "The Dressmaker's Child," a mechanic named Cahal is driving two newly married Spanish tourists back from a visit to a famous statue of the Virgin Mary on the outskirts of a small town. The statue is said to weep real tears.

The Spanish girl is very pretty. Cahal watches her in the rearview mirror. A girl like that, Cahal thinks, if I could only have a girl like that instead of chubby Minnie Fennelly. He watches the couple kiss fervently. They are either newlyweds or just about to get married, and some barfly in Dublin has told them they must make a trip out to the countryside to see "the weeping Virgin," that she would bless their union. And Cahal, even though he's pretty sure the tears of the Virgin are created by moisture in the air, has agreed to take them there for fifty euros, a good haul for such a short drive. And on the way back to town, as he watches them kiss in the mirror, a little girl in a white dress dashes out into the road. He's got no time to swerve. He hits the girl and keeps driving. The Spanish couple, in the throes of love, don't seem to notice.

Now this is horror enough, but because we're in a Trevor story and not the tired mind of a homesick Midwesterner in California, it gets worse. After seeing the white dress sprawled on the road in the rearview, Cahal remembers having heard strange stories about a little girl on this road who is known to fling herself at passing cars. This alarming practice has apparently been allowed to continue, and somehow, up to that particular evening, anyway, the little girl has never been seriously hurt.

Why does she fling herself into cars?

Cahal has no idea, and the narrator, whoever it is, never tells us. We only know that her home life isn't good and that her mother, a dressmaker, is a drunk and often leaves her daughter alone at night to go to a bar. There are other nasty rumors around town that the little girl's father is also the mother's, the dressmaker's, father, adding the threat of incest to a story that becomes increasingly twisted. Yet never gratuitously so. This stuff happens. We all know it happens. Think of all that goes on behind closed doors. Think of all that happens on lonely roads. But Trevor doesn't stop here. And his crime stories aren't crime dramas. There are always psychological elements that go far beyond plot twists. He is fascinated by intimate collisions between absolute strangers. In "The Dressmaker's Child" the girl's mother knows, somehow she *knows*, that Cahal, a mechanic, a guy she's never once spoken to, hit and killed her daughter on the road that night. But instead of going to the police with her information, she begins to personally stalk Cahal, haunting every move he makes—even invading his dreams. The tighter Cahal grips his secret, the more degraded his life becomes.

He had never seen the dressmaker close before. She was younger than he'd thought, but still looked a bit older than himself, maybe twelve or thirteen years. The twist in her face wasn't ugly, but it spoilt what might have been beauty of a kind, and he remembered the flawless beauty of the Spanish girl and the silkiness of her hair. The dressmaker's hair was black too, but wild and matted, limply straggling, falling to her shoulders. The eyes that had stared so intensely at him in the Cyber Café were bleary. Her full lips were drawn back in a smile, one of her teeth slightly chipped. Cahal walked away and she did not follow him.

That was the beginning; there was no end.

A friend of mine once told me that Trevor spends part of every year traveling alone. I think of him lurking in alleys, listening beneath our windowsills, hovering around in bus station bathrooms, collecting our dirtiest secrets. All the secrets we think we can hold on to forever. Sooner or later, William Trevor will expose them. And if you're not guilty of the one crime, you're guilty of another.

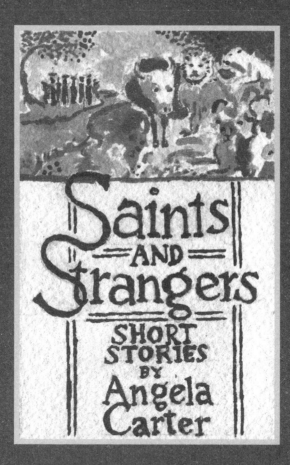

Saints
AND
Strangers
SHORT
STORIES
BY
Angela
Carter

CARTER ON BORDEN

Early morning of the fourth of August 1892, in Fall River, Massachusetts.

Hot, hot, hot . . . very early in the morning, before the factory whistle, but even at this hour, everything shimmers and quivers under the attack of the white, furious sun already high in the air . . .
—Angela Carter, "The Fall River Axe Murders"

I'm familiar with this Fall River swelt. My brother and I used to spend summers in a little house up in the Highlands with our grandparents. Everybody in Fall River likes to tell a Lizzie Borden story. Especially in August, when, as my grandfather used to say, the heat broils the toes in your shoes. My grandfather's Lizzie Borden story might even be true. He told my brother and me that he delivered *The Fall River Herald* to Lizzie after her acquittal, those years she lived up in Maplecroft, the mansion she bought with the money she inherited from her murdered father. Normally my grandfather would toss the paper on the porch and run like hell.

But one day Lizzie, or Lizbeth, as she began calling herself after the trial, beckoned him inside the house.

"Psssst, little Hebrew fellow. Come here a moment, will you?"

Grandpa Freddy was a well-mannered kid. He couldn't refuse a lady. He went inside the foyer. Lizzie Borden gave him an extra quarter tip, double what he made in a week. And when he told this story, and he often told this story, Grandpa Freddy would tell us again and again how her fingers lingered in his palm. How her fingers didn't leave his palm after she deposited the quarter, how they remained, skin on skin, for five, maybe even ten, extra seconds. And she wasn't wearing her glasses, her famous pince-nez. Lizzie Borden glommed her big eyes on his as if she were trying to communicate something beyond words, beyond facts, beyond the nursery rhyme repeating itself in my grandfather's head. My grandfather would drop a quarter in my hand (I was the youngest and most impressionable) and look mournfully into my eyes.

"Now scram, little Hebrew."

Then he'd gleefully sing the rhyme, the Fall River version:

> Lizzie Borden took an ax
> Gave her mother forty whacks
> When she saw what she had done
> Naked* she gave her pa forty-one.

Now, the intriguing thing about this genius of a song (I wonder who wrote it) is in the great unsolved mystery of the fourth line. The only mystery about the murder of Lizzie's stepmother is why Lizzie didn't kill her years before that August day in 1892. Because

---

*She must have been naked, this version goes, because no blood was ever found on any of Lizzie's dresses. The theory being that after she killed her stepmother, she burned her dress. Then she lay in wait, nude, for her father to come home for lunch.

she loathed Abby Borden's gluttonous guts and the whole world knew it. But it has always been undisputed that she dearly loved her father and doted on the man until the day he got axed.

I was seven when I cradled, in my own hands, those gashed skulls Grandpa Freddy insisted were the mortal remains of Mr. and Mrs. Borden. At that time these heads lived in a glass case at the Fall River Historical Society. I've been an aficionado ever since. A couple of years ago I slept in the room where Abby Borden was slaughtered. The place is now a bed-and-breakfast, Fall River's idea of a tourist attraction. To my disappointment, I slept great and awoke with zero new insights into the murders. I remember the quilt being especially cozy.

One writer who *has* shed significant new light on the story is the late British storywriter and novelist Angela Carter. Like Grandpa Freddy (bless his soul, he was a furniture salesman who died, in his office, at the age of fifty-nine), Carter recognized that Lizzie Borden was, like you and me, some kind of flesh and blood. The story is a steady, freakish march toward the inevitable. But the real brilliance of her telling is that there will be no carnage. Mr. and Mrs. Borden will make it out of the story alive. The bulk of "The Fall River Axe Murders" takes place in the early morning hours as Lizzie, her parents, and the servant girl, Bridget Sullivan, all sleep fitfully in the 80-degree dawn. And we are there, too. Up close. Very, very up close. In that terrible demented remorseless heat. Amid the intimate Borden household stink: ill-washed flesh, infrequently changed underwear, chamber pots, the slop pails, the inadequately plumbed privies, rotting food, unattended teeth. The smell of the Borden house is, Carter writes, "fit to make a sewer faint." And Lizzie Borden, the household's youngest daughter, readies herself for the day.

On this morning, when, after breakfast and the performance of a few household duties, Lizzie Borden will murder her parents, she will, on rising, don a simple cotton frock—but, under that, went a long, starched cotton petticoat; another short, starched cotton petticoat; long drawers; woollen stockings; a chemise; and a whalebone corset that took her viscera in a stern hand and squeezed them very tightly. She also strapped a heavy linen napkin between her legs because she was menstruating.

Carter revels in all the uncomfortable details collected by the court and Lizziephiles for more than a century. She's read all the books. She's read the trial transcript. She knows that two days before the murder the family ate twice-cooked swordfish that made them all sick. She knows that on Lizzie's dressing table is a bone comb with three missing teeth. She knows the titles of the books on Lizzie's shelf: *Heroes of the Mission Field*, *The Romance of Trade*, *What Katy Did.* She knows of Lizzie's great affection for pigeons.

She knows that Mrs. Borden is five foot nothing, two hundred pounds, and wears a hairpiece to conceal the fact that she's balding. She knows that skinflint Mr. Borden, a former undertaker, used to chop off the feet of corpses so they'd fit into the Civil War surplus coffins he picked up for a song. And also that, though he's rich now, Andrew Borden still waters the pear trees with his own urine to save money on water and has said, more than once, that he'd like to charge the cockroaches in the kitchen rent.

Back to back they lie, the miser and the glutton.

You could rest a sword in the space between the old man and his wife, between the old man's backbone, the only rigid thing he ever offered her, and her soft, warm, enormous bum.

The weirdness of the house is itself a character. It is a house of locked doors and private spaces, unspoken animosities, silent, boiling rage. Here people live on top of each other, and yet rarely, if ever, do they connect. There is also an especially peculiar architectural trait. There are no hallways in the Borden house. Just rooms after rooms that lead "in and out of one another like a maze in a bad dream."

Even creepier is Carter's description of a burglary that occurred in the house a few years earlier—and the principal reason for all the locked doors. *Someone* broke in while Mr. and Mrs. Borden were away, stole money and jewelry, ransacked Mr. and Mrs. Borden's bedroom, and then that same *someone* "pissed and shat" on the matrimonial bed.

> The perpetrator also wrote a few obscenities, in soap, on the walls of the kitchen.

The fact that Lizzie was found by her sister on the afternoon of the burglary, in the kitchen, holding a bar of soap, apparently didn't dissuade anyone from pinning guilt on one of those dark-skinned foreign infiltrators from Portugal. The other theory was that a poltergeist did it.

But consider Lizzie standing there, holding that bar of soap. Bewildered, alone, vulnerable, and above all—enraged. She's got nowhere to put the wrath. She's thirty-two years old. Fall Riverites already call her an old maid. And she plays the part. Lizzie's also a bit off, it is said. But up to now she has always done what was expected of her, according to the strict conventions that govern the behavior of her sex. She wears the right clothes (piles of them). She associates with the right people. She teaches Sunday school. She works diligently at charity for the poor. Two years earlier, her father sent her to Europe on a grand tour. She returned home with a reproduction of the *Mona Lisa*.

Carter suggests that the reason Lizzie Borden finally went over the edge and killed her parents was that Mr. Borden, not long before, had killed two of her beloved turtledoves with a hatchet. His wife had wanted to make a pie out of them. The most celebrated American double murder of the nineteenth century was revenge over a couple of pigeons?

Could be.

For what it's worth, my own thought is this: Whatever her motivation, she killed her father only *after* she summoned up the energy and hate to kill her stepmother. She *did* love him. Her last act of love was making sure he was dead before he knew Abby was gone.

But my theory is incomplete. How did she unlock the capacity to kill at all? Why that day? What combination of factors came together? The questions will go on being asked, which is why the legend of Lizzie Borden is so enduring. It's a bottomless story. At what point does anyone's potential to murder cross the line from inconceivable to possible?

The jury let her off because no man, officially anyway, wanted to assert that a woman, a daughter, was capable of carrying out what occurred in that house.

I think of how she must have looked to my grandfather when her fingers lingered too long in his palm.

In her old age, she wore pince-nez, and truly with the years the mad light has departed from those eyes or else is deflected by her glasses—if, indeed, it *was* a mad light, in the first place, for don't we all conceal somewhere photographs of ourselves that make us look like crazed assassins? And, in those early photographs of her young womanhood, she herself does not look so much like a crazed assassin as somebody in extreme solitude, oblivious of that camera in whose direction she obscurely smiles, so that it would not surprise you to learn that she is blind.

"The Fall River Axe Murders" is a story, not a diagnosis. Carter leaves us room to dwell on it, to re-create the mayhem in our minds. To be there. And beyond this, she accomplishes what, I believe, nobody has ever been able to accomplish before, and that is to finally give us Lizzie Borden the woman. It goes even beyond empathy. Maybe too far beyond. You get to feeling that had you been old Borden's daughter, you too might have, if the brew of reasons was right—money, jealousy, retribution, hate, love—in the demented heat of that morning, the weary flies droning, that stench, torn off your own dress and gone down to the cellar to retrieve a hatchet.

BERNARD MALAMUD

Rembrandt's Hat

SHAMELESS IMPOSTORS

"You talk to Dad?" my brother says. "It's Father's Day."

"No."

"You better call. It's our filial responsibility to recognize this patriotic national holiday. Otherwise fathers from coast to coast wouldn't know how much—"

"You called already?"

"Got it done early."

"How'd it go?"

"He was eating a grapefruit."

"Did he do the slurping thing?"

"Yes."

(Together, over the phone, my brother and I replicate the remarkable noise of our father eating grapefruit. Think of that tube the dental assistant uses to clear stuff out.)

"What else did you talk about?"

"Richard Nixon."

"Why?"

"You don't talk to Dad about Richard Nixon? What do you talk to him about if you don't—"

"I don't talk to him at all."

"Oh, right."

"What's he say abut Nixon?"

"He says he'd like to take back his vote for Humphrey in '68. He thinks Nixon would have made a great Democrat. One with some cojones."

Later that day I'm driving over Mount Tamalpais on my way back to Bolinas. The phone keeps coming in and out of range. Good time to call Chicago. Fathers and sons. They see themselves in us. While we run from the them in us. I speak generally. My point, I think, is that it's an intrinsic thing. You can't flee from those who carried you. But somehow we never seem to really believe this. We always believe we will outdistance our fathers.

Number one Father's Day novel? Hands down *The Brothers Karamazov*. A sampler:

> "Shameless impostor!"
> "He says that to his father! His father!"
> "Why is such a man alive?"
> "Do you hear, you monks, do you hear the parricide!"

But in the realm of the story, I declare the victor to be Bernard Malamud's "My Son the Murderer." To get to the bottom of fathers and sons, Dostoevsky needs 700 pages; Malamud can name that tune in under 8. All I have to do is think about this story and I become vulnerable to pathetic remorse. *All right, Dad, you've got me cornered, I do love you.* I dial. I almost drive over the lip of the mountain, but I dial. A phone number I know as well as my own name.[*]

---

[*]Now I call this number and a stranger answers. I hang up each time. The stranger calls me back and asks what I want, why do I keep calling?

"Hey, Dad. I'm driving in the mountains and so my reception isn't great, but I wanted to say—"

"Who is speaking?"

"Dmitri Karamazov."

"Oh, I remember you. The bedwetter."

"I've been thinking. Nixon got a pretty raw deal."

"You, too? Maybe we are related. One little breaking-and-entering and the man is crucified? Not like he was there, anyway. A piddly case. In Cook County that would have been at most sixty days and a hundred-dollar fine. At most. And if not for him going to China we'd all be wearing wooden shoes. You want Holland to be our largest trading partner? I'd take Nixon over this pansy-ass African-American any day. You think these Arabs are messing around? How are you? You need money? How much?"

"A thousand."

"What was that?"

"Three thousand."

"I can't hear you. The phone—"

"Five thousand!"

"Forget it."

My father did not say African-American. At the onset of his apparent senility he deployed an archaic Yiddish term I will not reproduce here. He did, though, say pansy-ass, which is a good word, combining a flower with a body part.

(Let me pause to announce that the characters and events described herein are either fictitious or, if real, used fictitiously. Any similarity to real persons, living or dead, is entirely coincidental and not intended by the author.)

But legal lingo won't protect this son. Or any other. Fiction or not, don't we become, eventually, one way or another, our father's executioner?

＊ ＊ ＊

In "My Son the Murderer," the son, Harry, threatens to kill his
father for opening his mail:

> If you do this again don't be surprised if I kill you. I'm sick of
> you spying on me.
>> Harry, you are talking to your father.

In this story, and probably countless others, to spy is to love.
Leo, the father, spies on Harry because he can't figure out what's
wrong with him. His boy is in pain and he can't do a thing about
it. "My Son the Murderer" is set in Brooklyn during the Vietnam
War. Harry has recently graduated from college. He mopes around
the house. He won't get a job. He retreats from his parents. Every
day Harry waits for his letter from the draft board. He watches the
news on TV.

> It's a big burning war on a small screen. It rains bombs and the
> flames roar higher. Sometimes I lean over and touch the war
> with the flat of my hand. I wait for my hand to die.
>> My son with the dead hand.

But Harry's anguish goes beyond, far beyond, the war itself.
His sorrow is as profound as it is inexplicable. He spends hours
hunkered in his room doing nothing, his father breathing outside
the door, listening to him doing nothing, trying to understand
what's so wrong with Harry. And notice what happened in the
above paragraph. There's an extraordinary switch in point of view
from son to father. From the son: *I wait for my hand to die.* From
the father: *My son with the dead hand.* Leo picks up where Harry
leaves off. He's watching and listening and trying to know his son

so intensely that his own thoughts bang off Harry's throughout the story.

I'm a collector of literature that depicts the myriad ways families don't communicate. In "My Son the Murderer," not only do the voices of the characters run together, but also—crucially—all that is unsaid.

At one point Harry does the best he can to explain himself to his baffled parents. "So why do you feel bad?" his mother asks. Harry replies, "I feel what I feel. I feel what is." And so Leo, the father, has no choice. He worries. And, worse, he keeps telling Harry not to worry.

> Harry, don't worry so much about the war.
> Please don't tell me what to worry about or what not to worry about.
> Harry, your father loves you. When you were a little boy, every night when I came home you used to run to me. I picked you up and lifted you up to the ceiling. You liked to touch it with your small hand.
> I don't want to hear about that anymore. It's the very thing I don't want to hear. I don't want to hear about when I was a child.
> Harry, we live like strangers. All I'm saying is I remember better days. I remember when we weren't afraid to show we loved each other.
> He says nothing.
> Let me cook you an egg.
> An egg is the last thing in the world I want.

My God, that egg. All the bungled love of every father in the world is housed in that egg. How many of these ineffectual eggs have I already offered to my own daughter?

Of course, Harry, we understand. Go on with your moping and your sorrow and your carrying the weight of an entire ill-conceived war on your skinny shoulders. Ignore your father's love. Shun it. Ridicule it. Stomp on it, Harry. Do your part in this age-old drama, this infinite dance of the fathers and the sons. Leave the house. Run away from your father and his godawful disgusting love. There will be no resolution, no solace, only heartbreak and irrevocable loss. But, even so, the father chases. Leo follows Harry on a trolley bus all the way to Coney Island. On the beach, the old man's hat blows off his head. And a son, an inexplicably sad and lonely son, stands on the edge of the ocean, water flowing over his shoes, and watches his father's hat roll like a wheel across the sand.

The Infinite Passion
of Expectation

Twenty-five Stories by
Gina Berriault

THE INFINITE PASSION OF GINA BERRIAULT

She was twenty-six already and none of the dreams had come
true.

—Gina Berriault, "Around the Dear Ruin"

I refuse to indulge in the senseless sport of ranking writers. Literature isn't rankable. It's us. Good, bad, moving, brilliant, tasteless,
shallow—all of it is us. Leave it alone, I say, with who's greater than
whom in this delicate endeavor of interpreting what it means to
be human. Why? Because there are invariably essential voices who
are left out. Consider those who conduct such rankings in the first
place.

An often cited example but one we might always keep on the
edge of our minds is that while Herman Melville was toiling in the
Customs House, trying to pay off his bills, J. T. Headley, Charles
Briggs, and Fanny Forrester were the toast of literary America. And
of American writers of the second half of the last century, who
hasn't heard of Gina Berriault's near-exact contemporaries such
as, to mention a couple of household names, Norman Mailer or
John Updike? Berriault didn't contribute very much commentary

on the state of our national affairs, and she never ran for mayor. Likewise, the brilliance of her metaphors never called very much attention to themselves. With Gina Berriault it is more about how acutely she penetrates into the souls of her characters. But isn't this the truest measure of our state of national affairs? The content, or lack thereof, of our character? That Berriault worked far away from the sources of literary influence doesn't make her work any less penetrating. She was a "quiet" short story writer and novelist, living and writing in San Francisco in the age of the Beats, Brautigan, and beyond. Over the course of many decades, Gina Berriault spoke almost exclusively through her characters, more often than not people on the periphery. After the publication of the collection *Women in Their Beds* in 1996, Berriault enjoyed a brief moment of national recognition. But, once again, her work is hard to find. Berriault died in 1999. As I understand it, she was an intensely private person who did not seek attention. My guess is she was working too hard at her desk to care very much about the business side of publishing. Every time I come upon a faded red copy of the 1982 North Point Press edition of *The Infinite Passion of Expectation* in a used bookstore, I buy it again. I like to have a copy in every room.

And another thing: Neither Mailer nor Updike, worthy as they are, has ever brought me to my knees with a sentence.

Place Berriault close to the top of any list of American writers of the latter half of the last century and she'll bring no shame, only subtle, devastating explosions of illumination. Everything clear now? I seem to be having an argument with myself in my cold garage.

The Infinite Passion of Expectation. You could make a case that this phrase alone captures the ambition and loneliness of not only San

Francisco but also our battered, eternally optimistic country. The passion of our expectations has always governed our days.

Knowing that these expectations will, for most of us, never be met in a single lifetime rarely limits our passion for the future. Thus our hope and our despair.

"Around the Dear Ruin" opens in a shabby studio above the Garibaldi Club on Columbus Street in North Beach. It's the late 1950s. A merchant marine named Leo Brady is just home from sea and about to see his new wife, the wondrous Clara, for the first time in months. Leo's illusions of a joyous reunion are quickly snuffed.

> My sister married Leo Brady because he was a merchant seaman and made good wages, and because he was gone most of the time. She and her five-year-old boy had been living on the sales of her cable car etchings that tourists to San Francisco picked over in the little art galleries and bookstores, and on the sporadic sales of her oil paintings. They were married a few days after he came from sea, and a week later his ship sailed again for the Orient. In the six weeks he was away, the steamship company sent her, at his request, all his wages. But the day that he returned was unrewarding for Leo.

Unrewarding. Very much so. On the day of Leo's homecoming, Clara is lying in bed. She's twenty-six and mysteriously sick. She refuses to allow either her husband or her brother to call a doctor. Clara has such a hold, love mixed with fear, over both Leo and Eddie that neither of them would dare defy her. She's in an extraordinary amount of pain, and yet, to the last, she retains her sense of humor. Between moans of agony, she advises Eddie: "Always remember to contradict your teachers. It makes good biography."

Clara is one of those people. Even in her final hours, she's a force of nature. Eddie and Leo can't take their eyes off the wreckage that used to be Clara Ruchenski. All they can do is listen, as Clara, increasingly delirious, delivers screed after screed. In one merciless diatribe, she describes Leo, even though he's right there in the room, beside her bed, black fedora in hand. He's wearing only socks so as not to disturb the patient by clomping around too much in his boots.

"How simple are his wants. All he desires is to identify himself with artists. He married Clara Ruchenski because she'd had an exhibit in some dank little gallery and sold a painting once a year. How happy he was on our wedding night. I thought people didn't get that happy anymore, not since before the Flood when everybody was a brute with a big, smiling face. No, no, I'm wrong!" she wailed, tossing her head from side to side. "I take it all back. I never did think like that about Leo. I'm not a snob. Please, Eddie," she begged, "you know I'm not. You know me, don't you, Eddie?"

Leo and I stood up.

"I don't hate him, Eddie. I mean I wouldn't if I weren't married to him. He'd be a big, sweet guy with respect for artists. That's the way I used to think, and I slept with him a few times, too."

A page later, Clara's gone for good. All that volcanic energy, and poof, silence. Leo, the new widower, takes a bus across the Golden Gate Bridge and tosses Clara's ashes into the gust at Muir Woods. Still, her voice echoes across the remaining four pages, and in my memory. Eddie tells us that his sister was terrified by the idea of obscurity and anonymity. It's easy to cast stones at Clara, but let's be honest, what artist—what anybody—can't relate to the fear of dying unrecognized. Unsung? Whether we're artists or book-keepers, how much of what we do will last? I'd like to believe that Clara is young, far too young, to believe in her soul that her dreams are going nowhere.

Yet "Around the Dear Ruin," ultimately, has less to do with fame or the artist's ego or even the work itself than with the people we leave behind. There's one moment I always have to take my eyes off the page to endure. Mark, Clara's five-year-old son, comes home from school carrying his little red briefcase. He stands in his mother's bedroom. Eddie watches from the doorway.

At first I thought that Clara was comforting him from a distance, urging him to come to her. But she was complaining about the Chinese boy who sometimes sits on a crate full of blue pigeons in front of a poultry and fish shop in Chinatown and, lifting out a fluttering bird at a time, cuts its throat while its wings stretch fanwise across his forearm. She was pleading with the boy to stop, her voice thin, bewitched, like that of a pigeon granted a human voice in the last moment of its life.

The kid is listening to all this with his face turned toward the wall. He doesn't know what to do. His mother can't even see him anymore.

After the fact, it emerges that Clara has had a botched abortion. As she ranted in bed, as her son stared at the wall, she was bleeding to death internally. Leo tells Eddie he can't understand it. He can't see why she would have wanted to get rid of his child so badly that she'd risk everything. We could have afforded nine kids, Leo says. Why in the hell didn't she marry Picasso, then? I'm always reeled in by Leo Brady's foolishness, by his steadfast love for a woman who never, for a moment, loved him back. Leo's just like Clara says, a decent lug of a guy with a big heart. The infinite passion of expectation.

"It's over me like a ton of water, the things I don't know," Leo says after meeting Eddie again, a year after Clara's death. Now, that does about say it. I hear you, Leo. As each year passes me by, I'm certain that I know less. Clara's dead, and Leo's still in love. Whoever she was or wasn't, whatever truths or lies are told about her, she'll always, now, be gone. But not gone too. That's the eternal thing. Grief: Leo's, Eddie's, Mark's, and yes, mine, keeps Clara's strength intact. Everything else—including the question of why I'll never shake her, this woman who lives for only a few pages in a book I'll put back on the shelf—is a ton of water.

THE ADVENTURES
AND
MISADVENTURES
OF MAQROLL
ÁLVARO MUTIS

TRANSLATED BY
EDITH GROSSMAN
INTRODUCTION BY
FRANCISCO GOLDMAN

SINCE THE BEGINNING OF TIME

Just before we got married in 2005 (M's family was Catholic; seven years of cohabitation was as much as they could take), I made an urgent trip to Chiapas, Mexico. For reasons I was never able to adequately explain to anybody, including myself, I had a notion that the Zapatistas needed my help to complete their historic leftist guerrilla insurgency. This crucial assistance given, I'd go back to California and become, of all possible unsuitable things, a husband. I took leave from my job and flew to Mexico. For a while, during my training for this mission, I stayed in a kind of expat flophouse in San Cristóbal, epicenter of the Zapatista movement. After a week of conversational Spanish, team building, and trust exercises, I was shipped out to what was called a Caracol, a self-governing area "in open rebellion," in the back of a truck hauling crates of oranges. At a checkpoint, I surrendered my passport to two well-armed and fiercely sexy revolutionaries in black ski masks. Long live Comandante Ramona and Subcomandante Marcos.

I spent the next two and a half weeks in a village in the mountains. My Spanish wasn't quite good enough to have many meaningful conversations with anybody, but the Zapatistas welcomed me with kindness and bemused tolerance. They'd seen my kind of gringo on the run before. My sole responsibility was to watch the road. I kept a daily tally of how many Mexican army troop transports rumbled by on the main road in order to intimidate the Caracol. When a truck passed (two or three per day), I'd run to the door of the hut where I slept and make a slash on the notebook paper tacked there. In theory, and in practice (years earlier, people had been killed in the region), my goofy American presence tended to act as a deterrent to violence. The army would shoot Zapatistas of any age, but, it was said, drew the line at glorified tourists in Bermudas and Ray-Bans.

Those two weeks, I also played soccer, reorganized the school library, hunted for snails in the river, and chopped wood. But much of the time, in my role as a human-rights monitor (I got a serious kick out of the title), I spent hours in a hammock reading a certain book left behind by a previous human-rights monitor. It was a collection of novellas and stories by Álvaro Mutis. A fat pink paperback with a spine so faded from the sun you could hardly read the cover: *The Adventures and Misadventures of Maqroll*. The book, which includes a story called "The Tramp Steamer's Last Port of Call," has become a part of my ever-growing list of can't live withouts.

His fellow Colombian García Márquez called Álvaro Mutis his greatest teacher of tales. And it was Mutis who introduced García Márquez to the work of Juan Rulfo when he personally handed him a copy of Rulfo's *Pedro Páramo*. And so books and stories move around the world, hand to hand to hand. Mutis was known primarily as a poet when in 1986, at age sixty, he turned a prose poem into the first "Maqroll" story. In the next five years, Mutis published six more Maqroll books. The nomadic, talkative, brazen, sometimes law-breaking sailor Maqroll has since become one of the most enduring and loved characters in Spanish-language fiction.

It's September 2013, and Mutis died last night in Mexico City.

There are two lines of the poet James Wright that I keep above my desk:

> Where is the sea, that once solved the whole loneliness
> Of the Midwest?

All morning I've been thinking of Álvaro Mutis in connection with these lines. As if loneliness were a problem to be solved. And yet this is the ultimate truth, isn't it? Aren't we perpetually, one way or another, trying to solve loneliness? The loneliness we feel? The loneliness we know is coming? Maybe this is what I was up to in Chiapas. For years I thought I must have been fleeing from a wedding that even then I must have known wasn't an answer to the problems M and I were having. Did we really think that the darkness that was closing in on us could be solved by a garden party in Olema?

"The Tramp Steamer's Last Port of Call" is a sea story about a seeming coincidence. The narrator, an oil executive who travels around the world, happens to see, at different times in his life, at various ports, the same boat, a dilapidated, wandering tramp steamer. It's as if this single boat has trolled the globe for decades, slowly trailing him. The image of the tramp steamer begins to haunt the executive. It becomes an obsession. He decides that this nomadic piece of sea trash must have something to tell him.

A sea story but, more than this, a love story. In Helsinki, the narrator finally (again coincidentally, but, as Mutis suggests, the very fabric of our lives is made up of these sorts of coincidences) meets the captain of the old tramp steamer and becomes privy to the story behind the boat. As the captain begins to talk, he tells the executive a story he's never told anybody. And he proceeds to recount what happened after he met a Lebanese woman named Warda.

I lie in my hammock and read. Across the field, the kids are in school singing revolutionary songs. For hours and hours, they sing. Meanwhile, two people fall in love, they fall out of love. The captain says not only is Warda gone, but so is the person he was when he was with her. Gone, he tells the oilman, as if both of us never existed.

> Before falling into sleep I needed desperately, I pondered the story I had heard. Human beings, I thought, changed so little, and are so much what they are, that there has been only one love story since the beginning of time, endlessly repeated, never losing its terrible simplicity or its irremediable sorrow. I slept deeply and—this was quite unusual for me—dreamed of nothing at all.

At the time, in my hammock, waiting for the troop transports of the Mexican army to shake the earth (I could always hear them before I saw them), I remember thinking maybe these kids spent too much of the school day singing. You can't sustain a revolution on songs alone. At some point, maybe some math and science might be in order. This from a person lying in a hammock. Now I think, Why shouldn't they sing? Why shouldn't they sing all day?

Onward, in my hammock, I sail forth. An old tramp steamer drifts across the oceans. A simple story, really. In the course of wandering from port to port, love's found, love's lost. What's more calamitous?

VOICES
from the
MOON

a novel by
ANDRE DUBUS

SURVIVING THE LIVES WE HAVE

A divorced father named Greg is not only sleeping with his son's ex-wife, Brenda, but now he's going to marry her. Before that, though, the hard part: he's got to tell the son, Larry:

> *Marry her? Marry her?* ...
>   "It just happened. It always just happens."
>   "Beautiful. What happened to will?"
>   "Don't talk to me about will. Did you will your marriage to end? Did your mother and me? Will is for those bullshit guys to write books about. Out here it's—"
>   "—Survival of the quickest, right. Woops, sorry, so, out of the way, boy, I'm grabbing your ex-wife."

The scenario is daytime-TV stuff, straight out of Maury Povich. And yet sensationalizing this would be easy. Demonizing the father and making a spotless victim of the son would be easy. Instead, Andre Dubus's short novel *Voices from the Moon* is a fervent meditation on the infinite variability of faith and love. For so long I've remembered this short novel as an unbearably sad story. From the opening line, "It's divorce that did it," this fictional family merged with my own. I know all about divorce. My parents. My own. Unlike my parents, mine was not only amicable; there were times M and I even laughed in the mediator's office. We felt ridiculous. There was so little to divide up. (Books, some coffee cups. M got that gorgeous sea-green Faber and Faber copy of Eliot's *Four Quartets*.) But divorce is divorce. It's a prying apart hidden inside a sheaf of paperwork. But this afternoon I closed *Voices from the Moon* and stared out the non-window of the garage. Wrong again: Remembering a book is like remembering a person. Everything changes when you re-encounter the flesh of the words themselves. *Voices from the Moon* is a joyous book. Hard-won but joyous, reverently joyous.

After overhearing this conversation between his father and his older brother, Greg's much younger, twelve-year-old son, Richie, thinks, It will be hard to be a Catholic in this house.

I'll say it will be.

The sentiment reminds me of one of Kafka's diary entries where he says something along the lines of: *Jewish? Now I have to be Jewish? I have enough trouble being a human being.* It's tough enough to be a human being or a Catholic or a Jew at any time, but when your father does something that makes your life that much harder—as fathers invariably will—what's a kid to do?

Rather than condescend to this twelve-year-old, Dubus endows him with empathy and wisdom. Richie is a deeply devout person who hopes to become a priest. Needless to say, his father's actions complicate his life. Richie sits in church on the morning after his father and brother have had their talk.

Beneath the host, Father Oberti's face was upturned and transformed. It was a look Richie noticed only on young priests, and only when they consecrated the bread and wine.

In movies he had seen faces like it, men or women gazing at a lover, their lips and eyes seeming near both tears and a murmur of love, but they only resembled what he saw in Father Oberti's face, and were not at all the same.

The last sentence above is uniquely Dubusian. It starts one place (Father Oberti's face) and suggests a comparison (the face resembles the faces of people in love in the movies) before rejecting the comparison in favor of the sanctity of the thing itself. For Richie, lovers in the movies were only *like* Father Oberti's face as he holds up the host. The miscomparison exposes and strengthens Richie's sense of the real thing. He recognizes that authentic faith is something different, tangible, while at the same time unexplainable in words—not unlike the love he feels for his father and his older brother.

Because Richie understands that we, whether or not we are fathers or mothers, will always do damage to our own families. All the faith and love in the world can't make us stop. As Brenda puts it to herself, she'd always believed "in trying one's best to be a decent human being whose life did not spread harm." But the book raises the crucial question: What happens when it's love itself—in this case, whom we choose to love—that causes all this harm? The sorrowful mystery here is not about how we might avoid spreading the harm. It is about how we behave in the aftermath of the harm. Do we compound it? Or is there another way?

Here I turn to Joan, Richie and Larry's mother. Two years before the story opens, Joan committed what many might consider an even more unforgivable sin against conventional morality. She walked out on her husband *and* her ten-year-old son. Now she lives alone in an apartment in a neighboring town. She sees Richie regularly, but the hurt never relents. Joan would rather endure, once again, the pain of giving birth to him than what she had suffered the day she told him she was leaving.

When Larry tells his mother the story of Greg and Brenda, her reaction is at once harsh and generous and surprising.

"We don't have to live great lives. We just have to understand and survive the ones we've got."

For much of the time I knew him, the last seven years of his life, Andre Dubus was in extreme physical and emotional pain as a result of the car accident that cost him the use of his legs. In his essay collection *Broken Vessels* he writes:

One night in the hospital I was lying with the light off, and I needed something. Maybe morphine or juice or water. I was about to press the button for a nurse when down the hall an old woman began to scream. She did not stop and the screams did not diminish in volume; they had the energy of pain. I did not press the button. I thought: You cannot ask for something when someone else is in pain. Then I thought: But there is always someone suffering, so I should never ask for anything. And at once I knew a saint would take that idea and run with it, would live that way. I waited until the nurse cared for the woman and she stopped screaming, then I pressed the button.

When I think of Andre now, and I think of him often, he was my mentor and friend, I think of the way he'd sit back in his wheelchair in his little kitchen in Haverhill, Massachusetts, and silently search my face for the sources of *my* pain. Sometimes he'd say, "Have you called your father?" Then he'd guffaw. Then he'd stop. "Seriously, have you? In weeks? Have you called your father? Here, use my phone. Forget the charges. Call him." Other times, he'd just look at me and sigh and grip his remaining leg and not say anything.

· · ·

THE COLLECTECTED STORIES
Isaac
Babel
INTRODUCTION BY LIONEL TRILLING

ZORA NEALE
HURSTON
Their Eyes Were
Watching God

EVERY GRIEF-SOAKED WORD

Having nothing better to do for the last couple of hours, I've been hunting through four different translations in search of a bad sentence by Isaac Babel. Such is the life I lead in this garage. Every line gets me in the groin.

> To live in Tiflis in the springtime, to be twenty years old and not to be loved is a terrible thing. It happened to me.

In another story he wrote this:

> Next morning, meeting the girl in the corridor, I hastened to inform her: "You must know that I have a law degree, and am reckoned a highbrow."

See what I mean? And there are thousands of such sentences, lines that leap to life, lines that make so much else you read stagnant. But all writers, no matter who they are, should be entitled to a bad sentence once in a while. Don't you think? How can a writer, any writer, know they're mortal if every sentence hits? Our bad sentences are the imperfections that light up all our others. To each our own bad sentences.

Babel addressed this himself in a speech to the First Congress of Soviet Writers in 1934 . He had no desire to speak at this phony literary gathering, but he had no choice. In Stalin's Russia, writers had to speak and they had to write. Writer's block was considered laziness, and silence by choice was worse: subversive. With his tongue firmly planted in his cheek, Babel told the crowd of writers:

> The party and the government have given us everything, depriving us of only one privilege—that of writing badly. It must be said frankly, without false modesty: it is a very important privilege that has been taken away from us and we took full advantage of it. And so, comrades, we declare at this writers' congress: Let us renounce completely that old privilege.

Even in that atmosphere, Babel went for a laugh, and he got it. With the benefit of gruesome hindsight, the quip works like a Babelian sentence. Brief, funny, grief-soaked. You laugh till your heart bleeds.

The man wasn't even allowed to live long enough to write badly.

In that same speech, Babel also noted the force with which Stalin "hammers out his speeches, how his words are wrought of iron, how terse they are, how muscular, how much respect they show to the reader." Maybe he was going for more laughs. Or maybe he was, like so many others, trying to save his own skin.

It is said that Stalin hadn't bothered to read Babel before he personally signed his execution order in 1939. The story goes that

Stalin phoned Ilya Ehrenburg (novelist, propagandist, Jew) in the middle of the night and asked him if Babel was as good as people said. Ehrenburg, bravely, it should be said, answered in the affirmative. "Pity," Stalin said, and hung up. But would it have mattered if Stalin had read Babel? People who on a whim can shoot anyone they want are incapable of reading well, because reading well, in my lonesome garage view, requires reading with generosity. If Stalin, a mediocre poet himself (beware militaristic, mediocre poets with power*), had read a little Isaac Babel, he might have experienced the shock of humanity. Would he have closed the gulags? Literature has never had much success interfering with the actual machinery of tyranny. Still, I hold tight to the belief that stories can, and do, stick it to authority like almost nothing else.

Sermonette over. I was searching for a bad sentence. Here's the best I can do. This is from "Evening," one of the *Red Cavalry Stories*:

> The night consoled us in our sorrows, a light wind fanned us like a mother's skirt, and the grasses below gleamed with dewy freshness.
>
> (Walter Morrison, 1955)

"Gleamed with dewy freshness"? Let's check another translation:

> The night comforted us in our anguish; a light breeze rustled over us like a mother's skirt and the weeds below us glittered with freshness and moisture.
>
> (Peter Constantine, 2005)

---

*Good a place as any to give a shout-out to the "warrior poet" Radovan Karadžić:

Goodbye Assassins, it seems from now on
The gentlefolks' aortas will gush without me.

Weeds I like better than grass, but "glittered with freshness and moisture"?

> Night comforted us in our miseries, a light wind fanned us like a mother's skirt, and the grass below sparkled with freshness and moisture.
>
> (Nadia Helstein, 1929)

> Night comforted us in our sorrows, a light breeze fanned us like a mother's skirt, and the grasses below glistened with freshness and moisture.
>
> (Boris Dralyuk, 2015)

All right, then. I'm not sure we can blame all this freshness on these underappreciated translators without whose thankless work we would never know these stories in the first place. And whether the grass glistens, gleams, or sparkles, it still clunks. Why not just call it wet? So we'll split the difference fifty-fifty. Call it a bad phrase within a luminous sentence. Because I'd saw off my right thumb to have written *a light wind fanned us like a mother's skirt.*

In the context of the story, the line is even more glorious. These two men lying on the wet grass are soldiers in the middle of a nasty war on the Polish frontier. They'll be lucky if they see tomorrow morning, forget about seeing anybody's mother.

I've been resisting saying anything about Babel for years. What could I possibly say beyond what Andre Dubus said to me eighteen years ago (has it really been so long since I've heard his voice?), when he lent me his copy of Babel's *Collected Stories*, with the caveat that I had to bring it back in a week. "Read it. Then get your own copy." It was a worn-out paperback, the old Meridian edition with the guy on the cover dressed up to look like Babel. That weird hat, those little glasses. This was before any photographs of him were available in the West. The impression you get of Babel is that he's a little Jew playing dress-up. A four-eyed bookworm who rides off with the Cossacks. I hoarded the book, read and reread it like a starveling. I broke the spine and was too embarrassed to return it. Andre called:

"Orner, you want to see *Mr. Holland's Opus*? It's at the Showcase."

"No," I said.

"Great, pick me up at six-fifteen. We'll get Chinese beforehand."

The cheesier the movie, the more Andre liked it. I remember sitting there in the dark watching Richard Dreyfuss forsake his own music career to become the beloved teacher his students would never, ever forget. I wanted to puke. Andre wept. He never asked for his Babel back. I have it here. Another thing I never had the chance to thank him for.

The strange thing is that I often forget what actually happens in a Babel story. I think this is because what actually happens is never, on its face, especially shocking. Death is coming, there's no getting around it; it either strikes or, at the very least, lurks in nearly every story. Something else I'm getting at, something more intangible. I think it has to do with the fact that a Babel story always unfurls in real time, so that to reread it is to completely re-experience it. It's like sex. Do we lust for it again because we're wondering how it will turn out this time?

He knew so much about us. He knew how relentlessly cruel we are. And also how, less common but still pervasive, gentle we can be. Attempts to categorize him never seem to hold. He's a Russian writer. He's a Jewish writer. He's a Jewish Russian writer. He's both and neither. May as well call him a Madagascarian writer. A Mormon writer. Call him a Delawarean writer. Why not? Because

Babel, like Chekhov and Gogol before him, can never be contained by ethnic, political, cultural, or any other cages.

This is not to say Babel wasn't utterly immersed in his own world. The poet C. D. Wright once riffed off Tip O'Neill's "All politics is local." Wright wrote: *All salvation is local.* Babel probably believed this. He did have one real chance to save himself. In 1935, he refused to remain in Paris with his wife and daughter because he couldn't bear the idea of not living and writing in Russia. If there was going to be any salvation, it was going to be at home, in his own language, among his own people. In spite of everything, his letters show he was wary, but also optimistic, about the Soviet future.

> The collective farm movement has made great progress this year and now limitless vistas are opening up—the land is being transformed. I don't know just how long I'll stay here. It is both interesting and essential for me to witness the new economic relations and reforms . . . The winter here is extraordinary mild and beautiful. There's a lot of snow. I feel well.

A Jew, a Russian, a revolutionary. I believe he was, as a writer and a man, inspired by the possibility of social change through great upheaval. He witnessed it all firsthand and was all too aware of the costs. But I don't believe he would have turned back to prerevolutionary days if given the choice.

Another way of killing time by myself here in the garage: I play what I call "Fun with Unexpected Literary Comparisons." And everybody upstairs thinks I'm hard at work down here on my *Mr. Holland's Opus.* The idea is to scan my shelves and piles and pair two writers with, *seemingly,* little in common. So, for instance, how about Elmore Leonard and Edith Wharton? Dickens is said to have influenced *The House of Mirth*. Leonard was once called the Dickens of Detroit. Hence, Leonard and Wharton: soul mates. See how much fun can be had?

For Babel, though, I've got to up my game. To choose an unexpected companion, I wouldn't look to writers like Malamud, Grace Paley, or Leonard Michaels, all who employ genuine Babelian rhythms, because, being urban New York Jews with European roots, these choices would violate the terms and conditions of the game, as they might be considered *expected* comparisons. You get the point.

In any case, to be serious here, the writer with as uncanny an eye and ear is Babel's near-exact American contemporary Zora Neale Hurston. Her sentences have a similar way of detonating in a reader's brain. And Hurston's fiercely individual characters—like Babel's—represent nobody but themselves. Both often write about isolated souls, underdogs, in conflict with the unruly rabble known as the rest of humanity. Both reported from deep within their own respective territories: in Hurston's case, the South, the Bible; in his, Jewish Odessa, the Revolution, the Bible. Both spoke hard truths to societies that refused to listen. Both were silenced. Hurston by entrenched racism and indifference, Babel by bullets.

> Then she saw all of the colored people standing in the back of the courtroom. Packed tight like celery, only much darker than that. They were all against her, she could see. So many were against her that a light slap from each of them would have beat her to death. She felt them pelting her with dirty thoughts. They were there with their tongues locked and loaded, the only real weapon left to weak folks.

In the face of all this hostility, Janie, in *Their Eyes Were Watching God*, never once stops seeing the world in her original way. All those people against her, packed like celery. If everybody in the courtroom gave Janie a slap, she'd be beaten to death. The beauty and comedy and horror of this line. Think about all those *light* slaps adding up. And just a page earlier, there's a sentence that would have brought Babel himself to the floor. Janie wonders how she will possibly endure the turn her life has taken.

No hour is ever eternity, but it has its own right to weep.

It will end. Somehow it always does. And people either endure or they don't. But this doesn't mean we don't have the right to weep. Possibly it is the only pure, inalienable right we have. Few places in Babel's work express Hurston's right to weep more emphatically than the 1932 story "The End of the Old Folks' Home,"* which depicts the powerless in conflict with an unstoppable modern force.

A band of elderly poorhouse Jews are working in a cemetery in the aftermath of the fall of the Romanovs. Amid the general euphoria, confusion, poverty, and wretchedness of that time, the cemetery workers make do by renting out a single coffin for repeated use at funerals. When you're hungry, you've got to make a living.

At that time timber was not to be had in Odessa for love or money, and the coffin for hire did not stand idle. The deceased lay in the oak box the allotted time in his home and at the service; but into the grave he was lowered in his shroud. This was in accordance with a forgotten Jewish law.

By itself the detail of the rented coffin is priceless. A lesser writer might have milked it even further for more laughs. But Babel never overtells a joke. The paragraph lands not on the coffin but on the

*Also translated as "The End of the Almshouse."

body wrapped in the shroud. That is: for dust thou art and unto dust thou shalt return. Who needs a casket less than the dead?

Things go wrong when a Jewish Bolshevik named Hersh is buried in the cemetery with the full honors of a revolutionary hero. As Hersh's division commander winds his tedious eulogy down, the Jewish gravediggers prepare to dump the body out of the coffin. The commander halts them with a nudge of his spur. "Move off," he said, "move farther away. Hersh was a faithful servant of the Republic." And so Comrade Hersh is buried in a coffin that had doubled as a cash cow. The old Jews don't take the loss of their livelihood lightly. With their canes and riding their wheelchairs, with their toothless mouths, they rise in protest. Their own bodies: as in Hurston, the only real weapon left to defenseless folks.

What could be more absurd? If in a revolution, as Babel wrote elsewhere, a mother is an episode, then who is more expendable than a few decrepit Jews? Babel's sympathies are clearly with these cemetery workers, and yet he also understands that the forward trajectory of history requires that everybody, including Jews, fall into line with the new world order.

A young doctor arrives at the cemetery. She comes, in the name of medical science, in the name of the future, to inoculate the workers against smallpox. It's Meyer Endless who starts all the trouble. He tells the doctor he's got nothing in his arm for her to jab. How can she jab him if he's got no flesh for her to jab?

In Babel, as in Gogol, as in Hurston, as in Welty, it's comic—until it isn't. Soon the old folks will not only be out a coffin, they're going to be evicted from their makeshift homes altogether. The cemetery itself will be nationalized, and the workers likely starve. "The End of the Old Folks' Home" is not preoccupied with suffering alone, and these Jews aren't stock victims. In Babel, inhumanity goes without saying. It's how his characters respond to the inhumanity that counts. Babel's Jews answer the Revolution with grief-laced humor. To confer victimhood on one's characters is to see them only as a type, as an idea, and people can never, if you observe them closely enough, be corralled into representing an idea. These old Jews aren't old Jews, they're Simon-Wolf, Doba-Leya, Arye-Leib, Meyer Endless . . .

"Life is a dungheap," Meyer Endless says to the doctor, "the world a brothel, people a lot of crooks."

And then God lowers the hammer. Hurston again:

So Janie began to think of death. Death, that strange being with huge square toes who lived in the West.

And Babel:

The sun sailed over the top of the green cemetery grove. Arye-Leib raised his fingers to his eyes, a tear oozed from the quenched hollows.

Collected
Stories

1948-1986

Wright
Morris

A BLACK BOY, A WHITE BOY

T wo boys are fighting. Neither is especially interested in beating the other up, but once these things start, sometimes you've got no choice but to go ahead with it. One of the boys is black, the other is white. The fight began in the schoolyard but has spilled out into town. Other boys are watching, moving along with the two boys, cheering on the battle. Unlike the fighters themselves, the spectators want blood. But by now the fight has become a dance. The red sun sinks farther into the flat horizon, and the two fighters become indistinguishable shadows. We're in Nebraska. It's the early 1930s. The black boy takes two steps backward and one step forward, swings and intentionally misses. Behind him is home. He's hungry, and tired from a long day at school. The white boy is known to be of limited intelligence. Actually, he's a stupid oaf. He's repeated the third grade multiple times. They had to take the drawer out of his desk so his knees would fit. The black boy thinks of the white boy as potato-mouthed. He can't even taunt right. All the more reason to beat him to a pulp. But what would be the point?

The white boy isn't thinking about any of this. He's only doing his best not to trip over his untied shoelaces. He checks the clock on the bank. How much longer is this going to go on?

Nobody is going to win. The dilemma is how nobody is going to lose.

The black boy's name was, memory knows this for sure, Eustace Beecher. The white boy *might* have been Emil Hrdilc. If they ever existed, both would have to be long dead by now. Even the school where all this began is gone. There's a highway there now. The fight itself is a half-remembered glimpse rescued from oblivion. It's a story by Wright Morris called "A Fight Between a White Boy and a Black Boy in the Dusk of a Fall Afternoon in Omaha, Nebraska." Wright Morris wrote upward of thirty books from the 1940s to the 1990s. Born and raised in Nebraska, he lived much of his adult life in Northern California. From Marin County, Morris dreamed of the Great Plains. Nebraska has a way of being overlooked, just like Wright Morris.

In "A Fight Between a White Boy and a Black Boy," two boys are engaged in something extraordinarily intimate. They are fighting, touching, trying to make each other bleed. Yet, for all the physical contact, each boy is having a separate experience inside the cage of his own head. It's as though the fight itself is an attempt to overcome what divides them. An almost ethereal silence coats the story. It's like watching a movie with the sound off.

The black boy has changed his style of fighting so that his bleeding nose doesn't drip on his shirt. The white boy has switched around to give his cramped, cocked arm a rest. The black boy picks up support from the fact that he doesn't take advantage of the situation. One reason might be that his left eye is almost closed. When he stops to draw a shirtsleeve across his face, the white boy does not leap forward and strike him. It's a good fight. They have learned what they can do and what they can't do.

Lately I've been returning to Wright Morris. I'm not entirely sure why Morris has been so on my mind, but it might be because he specializes in what I'll call inarticulate wonderment. No writer I could name builds his prose so completely around answerable questions. *Plains Song*, a novel I exalt with almost Talmudic holiness, opens with this question.

Is the past a story we are persuaded to believe in, in the teeth of the life we live in the present?

I find queries like this a relief. They immediately open out a story. Now more than ever I feel under siege by opinions masked as answers. I'm finding much of the talk I overhear—in the café, on the street, in newspapers, in magazines, online, and in too many books—more and more exhausting. Is it me? Or is there an epidemic of glib conclusions going around? Since when is everything so explainable? I've been rightly accused of early-onset curmudgeonry, but since when did everything become so coherent? The work of Wright Morris celebrates life as I experience it: a phenomenal muddle.

Teaching a seminar a few years ago, I remember saying that it is critical to always ask yourself *why* you are telling your story. What a line of bullshit. I've learned this at least. To stop making pronouncements. Stories need no why. They only need to breathe a little on the page.

* * *

"A Fight Between a White Boy and a Black Boy" sheds light on race relations in a small Midwestern city in the early years of the last century, but like any story written to last, it doesn't attempt any definitive statement. Only the image of these two boys, their fight like a dance, is indelible. I watch them. The black boy keeps edging his feet toward home, the darkened section of town. The white boy follows him out of a sense of duty. Two boys. Eustace was one. The other might have been named Emil. A single streetlight gleams at the far end of the block like a halo.

Late in the story, which is only three pages long, the focus shifts to another boy, the one who remained to watch this fight after all the other boys went home, the one who now, many years later, is remembering:

> Somewhere, still running, there is a white boy who saw all of this and will swear to it; otherwise, nothing of what he saw remains. The Negro section, the bakery on the corner, the red brick school with one second-floor window (the one that opens out on the fire escape) outlined by the chalk dust where they slapped the erasers—all of that is gone, the earth leveled and displaced to accommodate the ramps of the new freeway.

I wonder if maybe what we experience in real time is less powerful, less vivid, than our remembering it years, or even decades, later. This fight between two boys is recalled by a third boy, a bystander. Why? Why does this third boy recall it and tell us? Who knows? Because even though it was a fight, there was something beautiful about it?

* * *

I've driven through Omaha only once, and that was years ago, on my way to Chicago from San Francisco. It was three in the morning. I didn't even stop for gas. A few days earlier, I'd left my wife on the other side of an ocean. After landing in California, I had felt the pull of home, real home. I wanted to go and stand on the bluff at the end of our old street and look out at Lake Michigan. No hurry, though. My life was imploding, what did I care if I ran out of gas and had to walk a few miles? It was June in the Midwest. But I didn't set foot in Omaha. Now I wish I had. Imagine what I missed that summer night in Omaha. All the sleeping houses under the dim streetlights. Maybe they had something to tell me. Even so, I'll never forget a minor incident, a story that may or may not have happened there, in a town I didn't stop to see. Two dead men are boys again. The sun hovers just above the plains, the blood-red light. They're back in the schoolyard moving toward town. The other boys are back, too, egging them on. *Come on! Come on!*

Eustace only wishes this were over and he could go home to his mother.

Clumsy Emil's shoelaces are still untied as he shuffles through the dust.

Street of Lost Footsteps
Lyonel Trouillot

A SMALL NOTE FROM HAITI

The woman next to me on this packed bus is watching a Jean-Claude Van Damme movie on her laptop. I'm watching over her shoulder. Van Damme points a lot, shouts, scowls, does not smile. I'm thinking, This guy's not really that bad an actor. I mean, I couldn't do half the shit he does and not laugh. He's also got a cross around his neck, and it looks heavy, as a cross should be, burdensome. Van Damme bears the weight of sin and redemption. At the moment he is running across a roof while getting shot at by guys who are apparently rogue cops. My seatmate is wearing headphones, so I can't hear the sound. The whole thing is like a freaky ballet with guns and I can't take my eyes off it. I'm holding a novel—Lyonel Trouillot's *Street of Lost Footsteps*—but what's a novel, any novel, even this brief, hypnotic, feverish novel, compared to this goofball Van Damme?

This bus I'm riding is fifty or so miles outside of Port-au-Prince. I wasn't lonely enough at home? Not to toot my own horn here, but a guy who can feel alone on a crowded bus with an average of two people per seat has a certain amount of talent for it.

It's been comforting to watch a movie over someone else's shoulder. My seatmate's daughter is asleep, squeezed in the nook between our seats. We all introduced ourselves earlier. The little girl's name is Chantal, and she told me she's four and three-quarters. I said, Hey, I've got a daughter who's also four and three-quarters. I showed her her picture on my phone, but she looked at me suspiciously.

"Where is she?"

"California," I said.

"Why?"

"Because that's where she lives."

"Why isn't she on the bus?"

This stumped me a little. Here? I'm on an intrepid journalistic mission to interview an important Haitian writer. I can't bring my kid along while I'm out here swashbuckling, taking my life in my hands, once again, for the sake of literature. Reading my bullshit easy, Chantal tapped the photograph on the phone and repeated the question.

"Why isn't she on the bus?"

Her mother hushed her, and she ignored me after that. Then, during another shootout, she fell asleep. But just now Chantal has woken up and is tugging on her mother's arm because she's hungry. Her mom has paused the movie, and I'm taking this opportunity to take down a few cramped notes. Van Damme's face is frozen in contemplation on the screen. He seems sad, as if he wishes he didn't have to be so strong and decisive all the time. I've been thinking about the irony of enjoying Jean-Claude Van Damme here, given that Haiti whooped serious Napoleonic ass in 1804. Is Van Damme French? Woops, Belgian. French enough. Just don't tell the Flemish.

* * *

For the last hour or so we've been stopped at a roadblock. Chantal and her mother are asleep. A few moments ago the man in the seat behind me just knocked on the top of my head. Actually knocked, softly but determinedly, as if my head were an inviting door. I turned around and peered at him over the top of my seat. Sitting behind me was a small man in a black suit and fedora. On his feet were brown-and-white spats. He reminded me immediately of the silent little man  in the limousine in "Raise High the Roof Beam, Carpenters," minus the unlit cigar. Do you remember? Buddy arrives late to his brother Seymour's wedding. Turns out it makes no difference, because the groom's a no-show. Buddy finds himself in a crowded limo with an irate maid of honor, who, if she was to learn Buddy's identity, would tear his head off. Also in the car, though, is a little man with an unlit cigar and a gravy stain. It's only a cameo appearance. The little man never says a single word. And yet, for me, he's always been among the most vivid characters in fiction.

On this bus, a different little man in a suit offered me, clearly a lunchless person, half his cheese sandwich.

"Thank you," I said.

"You're welcome," the man said. "As soon as the officers are finished terrorizing us, we'll continue our journey."

So on the bus we remain. Two boyish cops, guns sagging off their belts, continue to scrutinize IDs. It's worse when they don't talk, when they just stare at the IDs as if they are hieroglyphs. Out the window, on the left, is a small lake; on the right, a steep cliff. In front and behind us, a line of cars, buses, motorcycles, women and men and children on foot. Chantal and her mother are still asleep. The computer has been tucked safely away under the seat. Money changers wave wads of bills. A woman walks beside the bus selling hats. She's wearing all her merchandise. I count eighteen sun hats rising from her head, and nearly declare myself happy.

I start reading *Street of Lost Footsteps* again and fall into it, completely. My sort of novel, one with the energy, momentum, and mystery of a short story. On a terrible night in Port-au-Prince, as the partisans of the dictator and the forces of the "Prophet" battle it out, the fates of four characters, a taxi driver, the madam of a brothel, and two postal workers, become intertwined. At the center is a love story that may or may not become requited. The two postal workers, hiding out at a friend's house, are doing their best not to fall in love as the mayhem in the streets moves closer. Who can think about love at a time like this? And yet, you know how it is: two people on the edge of love. The chaos outside is rendered practically irrelevant. Whether or not to fall for one another. Maybe it's an even tougher question than whether or not to shoot. In *Street of Lost Footsteps*, the vulnerabilities of individual characters reign supreme over the forces of indiscriminate brutality.

> We did not make love. I did not take her feet in my hands. I did not embrace her knees. We stayed in the bedroom without saying a word, embarrassed by its useless garden perfume . . . The telephone, the radio, everything was quiet. In the silence, the dream flowered in her eyes. In some way or another, we had led the night to us. It had followed us. Perhaps it was within us, and always had been.

The next morning, in his front yard in Port-au-Prince, as he chain-smokes and laughs and bangs his wide forehead with the back of his hand, Lyonel Trouillot will indulge a few superfluous questions about a book that speaks for itself.

Intrepid Interviewer: *Can you talk a little about Lawrence? She's a fascinating character because the narrator declares his love for her early in the book, but I get the feeling he doesn't know her at all.*

Trouillot: He doesn't! Listen, I don't have much imagination, and often I steal things from people's life. And those two characters in particular are very similar to people I've known. Lawrence is a strange character also in a way. What does she want? You don't know what she wants. Does she know what she wants? She's ordinary. But she should have that right, shouldn't she?

Intrepid Interviewer: *Of course, but by the end of the book, they do, I mean she does—*

Trouillot: Assert her own desires? Maybe she does, maybe she doesn't. I look at it this way. I'm always curious about what my characters make of their presence to the world. Am I just here? Okay, I'm here. There's no greatness in merely being alive. To be alive is something very ordinary. *What do you make of it?* Now there's a question. And in all my books, my people face the difficulty of making something of their presence in the world. The answer is always different. This is one of the reasons I always leave my endings open. Among the happiest moments of my life was when I met someone who had read one of my books that ends with a woman walking away, and she said, "I'm going to take off from the end and start a new book." I loved that because I had no idea where on earth my character was going.

3

AND HERE
YOU ARE
CLIMBING TREES

Always in the house of death, Virgie was thinking, all the stories come evident, show forth from the person, become part of the public domain. Not the dead's story, but the living's.

—Eudora Welty, "The Wanderers"

LARGO
DESOLATO
BY
VACLAV HAVEL

ENGLISH VERSION BY
TOM STOPPARD

MAD PASSIONATE TRUE LOVE

I behaved realistically, that is to say, like a coward.

—Václav Havel, "Article 202"

Last night, on New Year's Eve, the playwright president freshly dead, I read one of Václav Havel's plays in tribute. (Yeah, a lonely voice likes to party.) In *Largo Desolato*, a dissident philosophy professor fears being sent to prison, but also fears *not* being sent to prison. It's such a perfect Havelian situation. How fast it happens. Now Václav Havel, too, speaks with the fearless authority of the grave. But something else happened while I was reading, as the fireworks shot up from Pier 39. Havel whispered to me as if nothing had happened. He went on talking as if the headlines trumpeting his demise were all fiction. *Don't listen to all the facile tributes about my selfless, angelic qualities. There weren't that many anyway.*

The professor, Leopold, is the hero people have pinned their hopes on. Fellow intellectuals as well as ordinary workers are waiting for the professor to write something really juicy this time, something that will make the regime really sweat. The pressure is on, and Leopold falters. He's unsure what to say. The words won't flow. He complains to one of his girlfriends:

LEOPOLD: It's funny, but when I run out of excuses for putting off writing and make up my mind to start, I stumble over the first banality—pencil or pen?—which paper?—and then this thing starts—

LUCY: What thing?

LEOPOLD: The cycle thing—

LUCY: What's that?

LEOPOLD: My thoughts just start going round in a loop—

LUCY: Hm—

LEOPOLD: Look, do we have to talk about me?

LUCY: You love to talk about yourself!

I sincerely wish that this conversation did not so closely resemble those that often take place under my own roof. Havel himself once said that, of all his plays, *Largo Desolato* was the most overtly autobiographical. He went on to say that if he sometimes wrote harsh portrayals of real people in his plays, he always saved the roughest treatment for himself. A good rule of thumb for those of us who write about family.

What I appreciate most about Leopold is how unbrave he is. He spends much of the play furtively looking out the keyhole, quivering, waiting for the secret police to show up. When two cops do arrive, they are more comic than threatening. Still, Leopold seriously considers taking the deal they offer. All he has to do is disavow "a certain essay" he has written and they won't haul him off to prison.

There's an over-the-top scene when a young fan named Marguerite comes to visit the renowned philosopher. She loves his work, but more than this, she loves *him*, the man, the creator, and Leopold, in spite of his turmoil over the momentous questions, in spite of the fact that he may well be the conscience of his nation, lays the lonely-guy routine on thick.

LEOPOLD: Ah, my dear girl, I really don't know if I'm capable of love—

MARGUERITE: Don't tell me that you've never felt anything toward a woman—

LEOPOLD: Nervousness—more with some, less with others—

MARGUERITE: You need love! Mad passionate true love! Didn't you yourself write in *Phenomenology of Responsibility* that a person who doesn't love doesn't exist? Only love will give you the strength to stand up to them!

LEOPOLD: That's easy for you to say, Marguerite, but where would one find it?

(*Marguerite takes a quick drink, winces, and quietly bursts out.*)

MARGUERITE: With me!

LEOPOLD: What? You?

MARGUERITE: (*Excited*) Yes! You have given me back the meaning to my life, which is to give you the meaning back to yours! I'll save you!

(*Leopold strokes her hair.*)

LEOPOLD: You're wonderful, Marguerite! But I can't allow you to throw your life away on someone as worthless as myself—

There's an audacious honestly in Havel's work. You'd duck if you weren't laughing too hard. It's rare in most people, nonexistent in politicians. Ask any Czech and they might tell you that Havel, in his essays, could also be scoldy, lectury, unafraid to monologue, tedious, etc. And yet a good percentage of Czechs, I believe, loved him and were proud of him, even when they profoundly disagreed with him. More today than ever. So it goes with love and loss.

A Czech neighbor of mine in San Francisco, upon hearing the news and having no one to speak to who could truly understand her grief, went out to Golden Gate Park to lay a flower at the feet of the statue of another famous Czech, Tomáš Masaryk. Masaryk, the first Czech president, was also a philosopher, a man who wrote many books, including a groundbreaking study of suicide. Hand it to Czechs for electing thinkers. Can you imagine an expert on suicide being elected anything in the United States? County coroner?

As president, Havel had to make the choices he never would have had to make as a writer. A president, even one whose post was largely ceremonial, lacks the luxury of indulging too long in subtle arguments. The bombing of Serbia by NATO, which Havel backed, wasn't subtle. In 1999, I remember receiving an earful from my law students at Charles University about Havel being a hypocrite. The man who wrote "The Power of the Powerless" wants to murder civilians in order to stop a dictator? I pointed out that getting Milošević out of Kosovo was going to take more than an essay. Needless to say, my students had a point. For a man like Václav Havel to support the use of brute force rather than more humane, creative means must have been a tough pill.

But he was a man well aware of his own contradictions. In *Letters to Olga*, the unromantic collection of letters he wrote to his wife while he was serving his third and longest stint in prison, he's so candid you sometimes want to cringe. The letters don't always show the future hero of the Velvet Revolution/Velvet Divorce in the best light. When he was arrested that particular time, he was found by the police at a girlfriend's apartment in Prague. Havel responds to Olga's understandable coldness.

> You said you were not sending me a kiss and that I knew why. I don't know why! I do know, however, that you mustn't write such things to me—I felt miserable for several days. These letters are all one has here. You read them a dozen times, turn them over in your mind, every detail is either a delight or a torment and makes you aware of how helpless you are. In other words, you must write me nice letters. And number them, put the date on them, and above all, be as exhaustive as you can, and write legibly.

He also demands Olga do a better job of maintaining the country house, build up a more extensive library of philosophical texts for when he's released, and, for godsake, learn to drive. Model husband, no. Pain in the ass? Narcissistic? He's a writer. He's also doing time. At one point the authorities offered Havel a deal that would have allowed him to relocate to the United States. Havel knew it was a ticket to permanent exile. Havel, like Isaac Babel before him, needed to be with his own in order to create. He remained in prison for almost four years.

In *Largo Desolato*, Leopold muses about the writer he used to be.

> It was wonderful when nobody was interested in me—when nobody expected anything from me, nobody urged me to do anything—I just browsed around the secondhand bookshops.

This is the man who will lead the revolution? Why not? I'll take my presidents as I take my fictional heroes, flawed or not at all. Those who believe they've cornered the market on wisdom are the ones to steer clear of, in literature, politics, life. Give me the confused, the mistake-ridden, the still trying to figure it all out.

. . .

FREDERICK THE GREAT

It's only a dim memory of a conversation I once had with my grandfather when I was thirteen or fourteen. We were sitting in his study with the white shag carpeting and I asked him if we'd had any relatives who were still in Europe during the war. I don't think I said it directly, but I wanted someone killed in our family. What kind of Jews were we if none of us ever got murdered?

"Relatives!" my grandfather howled. "You want more relatives?"

And from behind his giant desk, he told me another story in the long family parade. A cousin of my great-grandmother, a widower and professor from Vienna, arrived in Chicago in the early 1930s. My great-grandfather Samuel set him up with some kind of job in his office, accounting, my grandfather thinks it was, but the facts are vague.

"A charity case; my dad was giving the man something to do while he got his feet wet, you know? He figured at the very least the man could count. Turned out he was a professor of philosophy. Philology? Maybe it was philology. What's philology?"

At the time my grandfather was in his twenties. Some relative shows up out of the old country. What's it to him? Anyway, the professor ends up loathing Chicago. He thinks it's a city of cretins, of philistines, or that's what everybody assumed he thought. Nobody could understand what he was saying. The man refused to speak English.

English, what does a man like me need of English? I speak the language of Goethe, of Schiller, of Rilke!

He returns to Vienna in 1934 and is never heard from again.

My grandfather, in that familiar position behind the big desk in his study, rubs his big skull and stares at me. My grandfather: a serial failure of a banker. That year he was at the helm of a savings-and-loan that went belly up. But he was resilient. Economic disaster seemed to buoy his confidence, not sink it. He said anybody who didn't know how to lose someone else's money shouldn't be messing with it in the first place. He'd get fired at one bank and immediately get himself hired at another. He'd say, Isn't this country a goddamn wonderland?

"But why'd the professor come here in the first place?"

"He must have seen the writing on the wall. When he got here, the writing over there didn't seem so bad, so he went back to read some more."

"But what was his name, Poppa? The man must have had a name."

"Call him Frederick the Great, what do I care? Forty-five years ago, the man stayed a month. The man wants to be a toady to Hitler, that's his problem. They probably flushed his body down the Danube. Another reason to be thankful you're a Chicagoan. In the words of the late great Alderman Krska: God Bless Mayor Daley!"

* * *

So I know only this: We once had a relative, a professor of philosophy or philology, who escaped to Chicago and found it wasn't much of an escape. So he went back home to Austria in 1934. I wanted a story with some meat, and my grandfather gave me a skeleton. I wanted a name. I wanted a connection. What did I know about anything? It's 2011. I'm still a fool, I won't deny this, but as my losses pile up, I no longer feel the need to look for them elsewhere.

NATIONAL BOOK AWARD WINNER

PARROT IN THE OVEN
MI VIDA

a novel by
VICTOR MARTINEZ

AN AMERICAN WRITER: VICTOR MARTINEZ (1954–2011)

When you fell down in the parking lot in front of the acupuncture clinic on Mariposa Street, you didn't have the strength to be embarrassed. The acupuncture was the only thing that eased the pain a little. But you didn't get embarrassed. If it had been me who'd fallen, if it had been me who'd been too weak to take a single step farther, if it had been me who collapsed on the sidewalk on a bright, ordinary October day, you wouldn't have blinked. You'd have shrugged off my apologies, my shame at being such an inconvenience, and pulled me right back up. When you fell, I hesitated. I looked at you on the ground as if you lying there was something I needed to remember, as if you were already gone, and when I was finally able to muster the strength to yank you up by the armpits, you didn't mention it. You asked how far the car was. You said, "Have time for a hot dog? The little stand on De Haro and Sixteenth?" It is a lie when I say I wish it had been me on the pavement, the sort of easy lie you detested. I wish it was me on the pavement. Because you were heavy. Because I was scared. Because I didn't want you to die on my watch. Because I didn't want to be the one to have to call Tina. This isn't much, but at least know I'm thinking of you now, today, on another October morning, and you're still not here. We lionize our dead. Vic, I understand that. It makes us stupid. But at least allow me this: I wish the car had been farther and that you and I were still walking toward it.

> *When I see my aunt's old dress in the closet*
> *where the soft tissues of her leaving even now*
> *drift in the vacant air, and when I remember*
> *how my grandmother's back would*
> *not let the coffin lid close, the sutures*
> *of my heart unpluck and their lives spill*
> *warm as urine through my arteries.*
>
> —Victor Martinez, from "Don't Forget"

• • •

The World
of Apples
Stories
by
John Cheever

CHEEVER IN ALBANIA

A woman is talking very fast to a man who is sitting at the table next to hers. I'm facing the two of them, trying not to make my spying too obvious. She's elegant and made-up, with a puffy face and large hoop earrings, and holds a very docile Afghan hound by a short leash. The dog is as exquisitely coiffed as she is; his tail curlicues upward like a thin wisp of smoke. The haughty dog doesn't give a damn what the woman is saying, but the man at the next table does. He's trying to be nonchalant about it—yet as the woman talks, he leans toward her and nods his head as if to say, *More, more, tell me more.* The listening man has a bullet-shaped, hairless head and is wearing a powder-blue shirt, with his collar pointing straight up. On the underside of the collar, what would normally be hidden but is now purposely flashed to the world, a line of inexplicable English: *Best Company òf Guys.*

It is riveting to watch people gossip in a language you can't understand. You're free to watch all the nuances of facial expression and gestures without having to worry about the substance of the gossip itself, which, we all know, is usually about the same thing. Who's sleeping with whom and who isn't sleeping with whom. *And listen, don't tell anybody, I'm only telling you this—*

I could have this all wrong. They could be talking about shampoo. Still, I'd bet the house I will never own that this has something to do with a juicy bit of local scandal. *Can you believe it? Those two?* I'm in Tirana, Albania. What I'm supposedly doing here doesn't need much explanation. Suffice it to say that I came here because I had an idea for a story set in Tirana. I used a raft of airline miles, and here I am. I flew Lot Polish Airlines. Lot is awesome, by the way; they still let people smoke on the plane. The NO SMOKING sign is lit, but the flight attendants don't seem to notice the drifting haze and that sweet old closed-in smell. But it's been two days and already I know this was another screwball idea. When will these notions cease? For weeks I felt that life could not possibly be worth living until I sacrificed for my art by heading, with godspeed, to Tirana to conduct essential research for a story. All I've done so far is spend money, and here I am in this café, loitering over cold coffee, watching gossips gossip in Albanian, as if the use of Albanian were exotic and out of place in Albania.

At the same time, I'm also reading a John Cheever story called "The World of Apples." I have a habit of avoiding books relevant to the given moment I happen to be living. *Go to Albania. While there, be sure to spend a good portion of your day reading about troubled WASPs cavorting in Connecticut.*

But the title story isn't set in Connecticut. It takes place in Italy and is about another displaced fool, an old poet, a New Englander who has been living in a villa in the countryside for the past thirty years.

> The beauties of the place were various and gloomy. He would always be a stranger there, but his strangeness seemed to him

to be some metaphor involving time, as if climbing strange stairs, past the strange walls, he climbed through hours, months, years and decades.

Bascomb is world-famous and habitually unsatisfied. The story opens with the poet swatting flies with a newspaper and muttering: *Why no Nobel Prize? Swat, swat. Why no Nobel? Why?* But the story is less about insatiable ambition than about what a writer does when he's simply got nothing left to say. All of Bascomb's best friends, poets of equal stature, have had the good sense to kill themselves before they ran out of material. Bascomb is befuddled. One morning he spends hours in bed trying to remember Lord Byron's first name. To try and get back to work, Bascomb quotes to himself Jean Cocteau, who said that writing poetry is the exploitation of a substrata of memory that is imperfectly understood. All well and good, but what happens when you've got no substrata left to misunderstand? On top of all this, the only thing the old widower can think about, aside from the Nobel Prize, is sex. Night and day, Bascomb reflects on sex. Consequently, the only poems he can muster up are lurid little ditties, pornographic limericks that he burns in the oven before lunch. Ashamed of himself, he flees to Rome where he goes to a concert but hardly hears the music. He's only got eyes for the soprano.

Something else about Albania now that I've come all the way here: I thought it would be cement-colored. Cement-colored and echoey and sad. Today it's July and cloudless. Much of the city is at the beach, I'm told. Who knew Albania had a coast? The story I had planned to write was going to be a cement-colored story. Behind me, in the ungloomy recesses of this well-lit café, are slot machines with colored lights that keep blinking on and off. WIN CASH NOW WIN CASH NOW WIN. There's also pop music, American songs sung in English by Albanian singers. I kind of like it. I'm pretty sure this is supposed to be "Bridge over Troubled Water."

My gossipers go on gossiping. The woman is coming to the moment. I can see it in her eyes. They are becoming wet with heightened anxiety; the best and most unbelievable part of the story is about to be disclosed. We're on the verge of revelation. She's trying to control the words that flow faster and faster. *Best Company of Guys* keeps edging closer, as if by his almost touching her she'll come out with it now—now—now. But the thrill, the ecstasy, is never the story alone but how the telling is wrapped. And when the telling reaches that point where there's no turning back, when it's all moving forward, when it's impossible to stop the sweet release—

Have I come all the way here to stumble on a lame metaphor?

She's told him. Now they both look a little depressed. The woman's face is less puffy now, as if the secret had given weight to her face that's now disappeared. Now she regrets having given away the goods in the first place. If she'd kept it to herself, the news would still be hers. The Afghan hound starts to fidget; he knows that any minute he'll finally be able to go home. His master is starting to get the sad look she wears at home since his other master took off years ago. *Best Company of Guys* is starting to pull away also. He tilts his cup into his mouth, even though he's long since finished his espresso. He lives alone also. It's why he spends so much time at this café. He says something basic, something like the Albanian equivalent of "It figures" or "Just goes to show you" or "It takes all kinds." They're wrapping the conversation up—and I know I'm projecting here (my whole life consists of projecting emotions onto other people while trying to avoid having too many myself)—but these two acquaintances have begun to think about how the story, the illicit (and now, to them, tired) story, relates to their own passionless lives, their own long trail of personal catastrophe.

Meantime, Bascomb just slept with his maid. This is a temporary comfort. Sex itself is not always better than thinking about sex, and thinking lasts longer. The poet's mind continues to be plagued. His poetry—gone. He spends an entire morning writing FUCK FUCK FUCK FUCK across page after page. Next, Bascomb sets off on a pilgrimage suggested by Maria, the maid, to a chapel in the mountains where he might make an offering to a sacred angel with the power to heal whatever it is that ails him. There's this awkwardly pitch-perfect line:

> All Bascomb knew of pilgrimages was that you walked and for some reason carried a seashell.

Nothing connects. I'm in Tirana. I'm reading John Cheever. The two are devoid of any meaningful connection. These are nothing more than notes written at a wobbly plastic table at the Las Vegas Café in Tirana by a goof lamenting another failed idea. Still, I'll always have loneliness. My only calling. And Bascomb, for all his fame, for all the legions of admirers who constantly climb up the steep steps to his villa to pay homage, is stone lonely. For his dead wife. For his vanished talent. And my two gossips are lonely. For each other, it's beginning to look like. They sit a few moments in silence and think of two happy people who shouldn't be—but are!—whooping it up somewhere behind the closed shudders of some hotel room in this sun-drenched ex-draconian paradise. Always better to be the source of gossip.

The lady with the pet Afghan hound stands. She tosses some change on her table. The change plings and the dog barks. Tasty Albanian kibbles at home at last. *Best Company of Guys* blows his friend and her dog a kiss. With his other hand, he twirls his empty coffee cup around his thumb. And Bascomb? Bascomb, who is as present in this café as all the rest of us lonelies? I watch these two, I read, I watch these two. And the whole time Bascomb is wandering and searching—for what he isn't even sure anymore. He treks across the Abruzzi lugging his lust with him like a heavy tail. At the chapel of the angel, he drops to his knees and offers blessings to his heroes: *God bless Walt Whitman. God bless Hart Crane. God bless Dylan Thomas. God bless William Faulkner, Scott Fitzgerald, and especially Ernest Hemingway.* Not the most original list, but Bascomb is old school, and how many American poets today would offer a special blessing to Hemingway? But it's what happens after the chapel scene that provides Bascomb with some actual relief. He comes across a waterfall that reminds him of another waterfall, back home in Vermont. He's a boy and he's watching, from behind some trees, as his white-haired father strips off all his clothes and dives headfirst into that brimming cascade. Back then it had confused him. What's his father up to? Why isn't he at the office? The middle ·of a workday? Buck naked?

> Now he did what his father had done—unlaced his shoes, tore
> at the buttons of his shirt, and knowing that a mossy stone
> or the force of the water could be the end of him he stepped
> naked into the torrent, bellowing like his father.

It comes to me now. When I was eleven or twelve, I used to spend a lot of time under a little bridge that extended over the ravine in our neighborhood. One day, I was down there, lying in the dead leaves, and murdering the inchworms that liked to crawl up the underside of the bridge, when I overheard two neighbors talking above me. One neighbor, Mrs. Gerstad, referred to a certain married woman who often walked her dog at night in order to rendezvous with a certain married man also walking his dog.

"I don't believe a word," Mrs. Krasner said.

"Corner of Sylvester and Hazel," Mrs. Gerstad said. "You know the little stand of trees near the Preskills'?"

"Oh, Donna, really. Walking their dogs?"

I can still hear Mrs. Gerstad's voice, so viscously excited she could hardly get the words out. "Own two eyes, Helen. Barely keep their clothes on. Dogs get a show, I tell you—"

"No!"

I have always remembered that I felt shame under that bridge. Here's another possibility. It might even be the truth. Thinking about Mrs. Gerstad and Mrs. Krasner again today, let me say that I now remember—in vivid cement colors—that I was happy for my mother. I was ten or eleven, but I thought, Good for her. Mom has seemed a little lighter on her feet lately. This may turn out to be one of the most inspired moments of my life. Mom figured it out. Fuck it. Why not be happy? At least try? It's our previously misunderstood memories that give us our content, said a very avant-garde Frenchman.

OVERHEAD IN A BALLOON

Stories of Paris

MAVIS GALLANT

ALL LIVES ARE INTERESTING

My father lies, at this moment, in a bed in a rehabilitation center outside Chicago. He's very confused; he's not sure why he's there. At times he seems to think he's still married to my mother. The other day, over the phone, he complained about her taste in furniture. Today he told me he was locked out of his hotel room and only my mother had the key.

"She's out playing tennis," he said.

"Who's playing tennis?"

"Your mother. She's out playing doubles with the Berncrandts and that fool Barney Moss."

"My mother who?"

"You don't know who your mother is?"

My parents divorced in 1983.

And then: moments of lucidity and rage, terrifying because of how short-lived they are, because of how quiet he suddenly gets, as if he's aware of how useless anger is now. The anger that used to get him so far. And now I sit here, two thousand miles away, because I've got a life to live with my own family and my work and my massive credit-card bill, and I'm free and easy in my guilt, reading stories about other people dying in the hope that they will rescue something in me, something in him.

I've always had such faith in stories. It's a little ridiculous. Today the sky over Bolinas reminds me of my father's powder-blue eyes, and I find myself listening to the birds and the noise of a distant chain saw, weirdly happy. What is it about the sound of a chain saw that can do that?

This morning, hours before I heard the news that she was gone, I read an essay by Mavis Gallant called "Paul Léautaud, 1872–1956." It's about a now obscure writer once known in French literary circles as the Great Insulter. In her essay, Gallant sets out to resurrect him.

> All lives are interesting; no one life is more interesting than another. It all depends on how much is revealed and in what manner.

It's not much of a coincidence that I happened to be reading Gallant on the morning of her death, because I often read Gallant in the morning before I start to work. She sets the bar so high I can relax in the knowledge that, whatever I say, I'll never be able to say it as lucidly as she does. I think of all the mornings I read her while she was still alive, in Paris, prowling the streets and taking the notes that led to the creation of a galaxy of stories. Alive, dead, what's it matter to me? A single person who gave life to so many everlasting characters? I had her books then, I have her books now. Let others shout her praises today from the rooftops. Mavis Gallant is all days. And maybe all deaths are uninteresting because, ultimately, they all create the same silence?

* * *

But yes, lives. All *lives* are interesting. Gallant tells us that Paul Léautaud, for instance, could not stand any sort of grandiloquence in writing. In particular, he loathed the word "inspiration." He was a broke, blunt writer who managed in his eighty years to alienate anybody who got anywhere near him. Once, after rejecting a literary prize, Léautaud wrote: "Any writer who accepts an award is dishonored." Publishers dumped him. Editors stopped giving him work. The only ones who stuck with Léautaud were a few loyal readers.

> Even at his most caustic there was a simplicity, an absence of vanity, rare in a writer. He talked about death and love, authors and actors, Paris and poetry, without rambling, without moralizing, without a trace of bitterness for having fallen on hard times. He was sustained, without knowing it, by the French refusal to accept poverty as a sign of failure in an artist.

The French refusal to accept poverty as a sign of failure. Is there anything more blazingly un-American than this? It's enough to make me want to go back and study the French I never studied in high school. Because one human being *is* a kind of nation-state. The essay demonstrates how incisively Mavis Gallant saw into the souls of other people, who, when all is said and done, are often as distant from us as other countries. In story after story after story, Gallant slashes that distance and allows us, her readers, not just to know other people, but also to become them. Their wounds become our wounds.

If Gallant's take on Léautaud is a radiant look at an actual writer, her story "In Plain Sight" is among her great stories about a fictional one. Henri Grippes's best days are long behind him. One of the recurring jokes in the story is that Grippes is so old that no one dies in his novels anymore. It would cut too close to the bone.

We meet the ancient novelist moping in his Paris apartment, when the weekly air-raid siren goes off. The siren reminds him of the not-so-distant war, which in turn reminds him of his relationship with Mme. Parfaire, the upstairs neighbor he hasn't exchanged a word with in years. Gallant understood that mostly what we humans do is daydream, that while we're going about the business of our lives in one direction, we're daydreaming it away in another. Six years earlier, Mme. Parfaire offered herself to Grippes in one swoop—as a roommate, as a friend, as a lover. Grippes turned her down in the cruelest way possible while standing in the hallway outside his apartment door. The writer in me, reading Grippes's rambling diatribe of a response to Mme. Parfaire, only wants to stand in awe. It is so remorseless as to be miraculous. *Ah, so this is how you pivot a story. Unhinge someone, and then just step back and watch and listen.* As a human being, I want to step in and do something. Henri, you indifferent prick. Mme. Parfaire is offering you the rest of her life. She isn't even insisting you get married. At least offer the woman a cup of coffee. As it was, all I could do was catch my breath and listen to the elevator.

> The only sound, once Grippes had stopped speaking to Mme. Parfaire, was the new elevator, squeaking and grinding as if it were very old.

And yet as keenly as we see him, Grippes remains mysterious to himself. You'd think he'd try to make some sense of his life in old age, death impending, but everything only becomes more confusing. The fact that he's a writer, someone who, theoretically at least, is supposed to be self-reflective, doesn't help an iota. Amen to this. Gallant's characters fly in the face of that question that often plagues books about writing: *What does your character want?* Because she's honest about the simple truth that most people, Grippes included, have no clue what they want. He's just trying to make it through another day without falling into a memory pit.

Do you know what you want? I don't know what I want. Depends on the how, depends on the day.

At a time when so many writers are turning inward (including this one), Gallant reminds us that fiction writers must—in order to create lasting characters—imagine people who are as inconsistent, as foolish, as rash as we are out here beyond the page.

In the essay, she notes that Paul Léautaud had planned out his last words. They were supposed to be: "I regret everything." On his deathbed, he changed his mind and muttered something else. *Foutez-moi la paix*, which translates somewhat roughly as: Leave me the hell alone.

What two French writers, one real, one fictional, and my father have to do with one another, who knows? It's something only Mavis Gallant could untangle. For forty-five years, every day, my father sat in his office on the thirty-second floor of the American National Bank building on North LaSalle Street and practiced insurance defense. Or, as he put it, *I'm a connoisseur of slip and fall.* One of my father's claims to fame was that he was among the first Jewish lawyers to represent State Farm Insurance. Before him, he used to say, they wouldn't let a Jew anywhere near the golf course where they did all their business. He loved practicing law, and I think of him with one leg thrown over his office chair bellowing at secretaries, other lawyers, even his own father. When my nearly bankrupt, pensionless, seventy-nine-year-old grandfather lost his job for the last time, my father took him in, and though he did it out of love—he must have, there must have been love—he also didn't let my grandfather forget the charity and often sent him out on errands, as if he were a file clerk. *Dad! Dad! Coffee! ASAP!*

From a distance, all dementia is the same. Up close, it's personal. Everything you thought was buried gets dug up, and there, suddenly, it is. My father quietly, desperately asking: *Where's your mother?* What? Did he finally have something to say to her? I've never thought of writing as cathartic. It's work. I love it, but it's work. But I do believe that sometimes we need, in whatever way we can muster, to share our burdens. And a reader, a stranger—you reading this—somehow you make the weight a little easier to carry.

Mavis Gallant, understander of souls, is dead in Paris. On the same morning my father stares at a TV without seeing it. I call him up. I tell him he has to eat, I tell him to listen to the physical therapist. Some moments he's calm. Others he's terrified and begins, again, to panic. Still, he's an attorney, founding partner at Orner and Wasserman.

"Eric—"

"Peter," I said.

"Whichever, look, let me tell it to you straight, no bullshit, direct from the horse's mouth: I don't have any idea where in hell I even am."

Me, I'm in California listening to a chain saw.

· · ·

SAUL BELLOW

MOSBY'S MEMOIRS AND OTHER STORIES

Six amazing characters
with six remarkable
stories to tell

Ben Shahn

SISTERS AND BROTHERS

In the last days of her life, my aunt, my father's only sibling, refused to let him visit her hospital room. After numerous attempts, my father gave up. My aunt died without the two of them exchanging a word. The next time they met was at my aunt's open casket. She couldn't keep him away from her then.

Saul Bellow once probed a similar heartbreak. A decades-long rift, an immovable sister, an imploring brother who wants only to say goodbye. In "The Old System," Isaac has been trying for years to reconcile with his sister, Tina. Every Yom Kippur he arrives at her house to offer (as well as beg for) forgiveness. Just before she slams the door, he says:

> "Tina! For God's sake, I've come to make peace."
> "What peace! You swindled us out of a fortune."

When Tina becomes seriously ill with cancer, she continues to refuse to see Isaac, and Isaac, in turn, becomes increasingly desperate to say goodbye. The standoff continues. Tina won't budge.

"Why should I? A Jewish deathbed scene, that's what he wants."

Finally, after weeks back and forth, she relents. Tina sends a message through another brother, Mutt. All right, tell him I'll see him, but it will cost the bastard a grand.

Isaac hesitates. A bribe to see a dying sister? Is it kosher? He consults a rabbi in Brooklyn who says, *Why not? What's money if you've got money?* Isaac lugs the cash to the hospital stuffed in a briefcase.

No such payoff in my family. Even if my father had gone to the length of offering my aunt money, she still wouldn't have agreed to see him. With us there was no high drama, no operatic hysteria. Just silence. We're postmodern Jews. Post-Jew Jews. Urbane, fully dulled Americans. We didn't go in for this shtetl sort of stuff. It was the 1990s. The same inexplicable, ancient malices persisted, but you didn't make a public ruckus.

"She doesn't want to see me," my father said, "the woman doesn't have to see me. Free country."

In "The Old System" this other brother and sister, Tina and Isaac, come back to life via the memory of a surviving cousin who is sitting at the kitchen table looking out the window. This is my preferred species of story, a kitchen table story, where a single, motionless narrator looks out a kitchen window and ponders. If I could get away with trying to write such stories for the rest of my life, I would, because I believe in kitchen table silence.

It was a thoughtful day for Dr. Braun. Winter. Saturday. The short end of December. He was alone in his apartment and woke late, lying in bed until noon, in the room kept very dark, working with a thought—a feeling: Now you see it, now you don't.

Nothing about this particular morning sends Dr. Braun back to the past, unless it is something about the already fading afternoon light. Bellow refuses to create any false cause and effect. Dr. Braun remembers his cousins today because he happens to remember them today. He looks out across the alley at the circular tank of a laundry. He feels a "sentiment approaching" and suddenly thinks, No, it isn't true, what was said of him, that he didn't love anyone. Rather, he didn't love anyone steadily. But unsteadily he loved, Dr. Braun guessed, "at an average rate."

> They were dead. Isaac Braun and his sister Tina. Tina was the first to go. Two years later, Isaac died. Braun now discovered that he and Cousin Isaac loved each other. For whatever use or meaning this fact might have within the peculiar system of light, movement, contact, and perishing in which he tried to find stability. Toward Tina, Dr. Braun's feelings were less clear. More passionate once, but at present more detached.

Dr. Braun remembers Isaac standing under a sycamore tree at the Brauns' summer place up in the Mohawk Valley of New York. He remembers that they used to call tadpoles polliwogs. And he remembers Tina coming to his bed when he was recovering from a bee sting and lifting up her dress. And as Dr. Braun continues to drink his coffee and look out the window at the icicles hanging off the tank across the alley, Isaac and Tina emerge, alive and well, as teenagers, then young adults. The years lurch forward. Eventually, his two cousins fall out over money. Isaac builds malls and cheap apartment buildings by the dozens. Tina accuses Isaac of fleecing her out of her inheritance in order to build his real estate empire.

Not only does Dr. Braun sit and think, but he also invents thoughts and dialogue for the cousins he's remembering. As with Chekhov's dying bishop, Dr. Braun is a character retrieving the lives of *other* characters only he remembers.

> Isaac's Orthodoxy only increased with his wealth. He soon became an old-fashioned Jewish paterfamilias . . . He, too, kept the Psalms near. As active, worldly Jews for centuries had done. One copy lay in the glove compartment of his Cadillac. To which his great gloomy sister referred with a twist of the face. . . . She said, "He reads the Tehillim aloud in his air-conditioned Caddy when there's a long freight train at the crossing. That crook! He'd pick God's pocket!"

This is how we'll be remembered down the line, as caricatures in the mind of a surviving family member. How is it that living relatives like Dr. Braun are entrusted with the sacred memory of our dead? The answer (and this might be the only thing in this book that I'm absolutely certain of): *Who in the hell else would bother with our dead?* This is what "The Old System" does so unapologetically. It is a story that hinges completely on the simple idea of bothering to remember.

Both my aunt and my father are buried with my grandparents, but as far away from each other as geometrically possible within the confines of the sad rectangle that constitutes our family plot in Skokie. An abyss separates these two Orners. If they were granted resurrection tomorrow, would they ever speak again? I wonder. I look to Tina and Isaac Braun to experience the peace my father and his sister never made. The source of their Balkan-like loathing, no one will ever know, but it had something, the story has always gone, to do with my father's resentment that his sister received more attention from my grandmother while my grandfather was off fighting the Japanese in the South Pacific.

Huh?

This dubious explanation has reigned as unquestioned family gospel for the last sixty years. And, of course, this World War II story addresses only half of it, because it doesn't attempt to elucidate what my aunt had against my father, unless it is merely that hate begets hate. In any case, the story will be told as long as those who remember my father and my aunt are still alive. In a couple of decades, we'll be down to a handful.

Henry James once wrote that fiction isn't what happened but what should have happened. I hadn't understood what he meant by this until I applied the idea to this rift in my own family. In Bellow's story, what should have happened *happened*. As Dr. Braun remembers it, sister and brother come together. Tina and Isaac enact their tearful goodbye, and if it costs them, it costs them. The story gains everything by bringing the two warring siblings together. We get the scene, and all the pain Bellow puts his characters through becomes, in a sense, worth every extorted dollar. Fiction embodies life. What should have happened.

"Tina!"

"I wondered," she said.

"It's all there."

But she swept the briefcase from him and in a choked voice said, "No. Take it." He went to kiss her. Her free arm was lifted and tried to embrace him. She was too feeble, too drugged. He felt the bones of his obese sister. Death. The end. The grave. They were weeping.

For my aunt and my father: lifelessness. It will always be too late, and yet: there are times, like now, when I sit and remember (with an almost giddy feeling) how they used to glare at each other across the dinner table at my grandparents' house on Pine Point Drive. Was there some sort of mutual fascination in that glaring? They never exchanged more than a few words, never conversed. My father would mutter something under his breath like, Why'd you chop your hair all off? Eventually, my aunt would throw her napkin down, ease off her chair, and laugh, a high false laugh, as she stalked out of the room. "Go to hell, Ronnie," she'd say over her shoulder. My aunt was the only one who ever called him Ronnie.

HEINRICH BÖLL

18 STORIES

PARTING

It wasn't visiting hours. They let me in, anyway, after I begged from a wall phone on the first floor of the hospital. M was on the fifth floor. I needed a special code to work the elevator. After I buzzed, I was led through two locked doors and down a long corridor before entering the TV room, which doubled as a lunchroom. M was sitting there on a bench, holding a book. Her eyes were so calm, so calm that I worried. Who knows what the title of the book was, for once I didn't care, but I do remember staring at the cover. It had a drawing of an ornate iron gate. Beyond the gate was a gray sea. I sat down next to M. She laughed and told me about a guy who earlier that morning had called his mother from the public phone and shouted, loud enough the entire floor could hear: *Please, Mom, get me out of here so I can kill myself in peace.* M pointed to a boy—he couldn't have been more than sixteen—sitting at one of the lunch tables listening to headphones, quietly drumming the table with his palms.

"That's him," M said. "He'll be all right."

"You'll be all right, too," I said.

"You know, I've been thinking, maybe it doesn't really matter."

"Of course it does. You will. Soon. It's just going to take—"

"I'm trying."

"Good."

"Trying to try, anyway."

"You've just got to keep—"

"Let's not start. All right?"

I looked around the room. In the corner was a pile of tattered boxes of board games. Sorry, Connect Four, Risk. There was a stack of year-old *Newsweeks*. There was a computer inside what looked like a video arcade game, the screen behind thick glass, a keyboard dangling from a chain.

"I brought you a brownie," I said, and handed her the little paper bag.

We used to say we lived in the country of us. I've never been able to explain this, though everyone I have ever told has always nodded like they understood. But how could they? Years of mornings, years of nights. I watched M eat the brownie. I used to read her my stories. The minute I finished one I'd beg her to listen and she'd sit on the couch and listen with her feet tucked under her legs and her chin in her hands, and if a line ran wrong, she'd lift her head slightly, only slightly, but enough so I'd notice, and I'd make a mark by that sentence because I knew right there I'd blown it.

"They let us wear our own clothes, thank God."

"You're too thin," I said.

"How's your daughter?"

"Let's not—"

"I'm asking."

"Good. Still not sleeping that much, but that's—"

"Right. That's how it goes. You forget I basically raised two little brothers? Brownie?"

"I brought it for you."

"Take some," she said.

The boy at the lunch table turned up the music in his ears so that we could hear the tinny beats from where we were sitting.

"Don't write about me," she said.

"How do you know?" I said.

"I can tell. You look guilty."

"I'm not writing about you, I'm writing about us."

"Us?"

"Right."

"Us, us? Or us as in a fictional construct based—"

"Us us. Just a few pages. I couldn't get myself to say very much. I didn't know what or even how—"

A man came in. He was wearing a long coat. He tried to make the computer work. After pressing a few buttons on the keyboard, he began banging it with his fists.

"He works here," M whispered. "He's more batshit than anybody. Don't use my name."

"Okay."

"Nobody would be able to pronounce it, anyway."

"Right."

"Can I read it?"

"Of course."

"Use an initial."

"Okay."

"Like in those old stories where the character doesn't have a name, just a letter signifying—"

"All right."

"A mysterious presence. Towns, they do it with towns, also,

don't they? T arrived in S after midnight. It was raining. Didn't know a soul, just carried with him an address scrawled on a train ticket—"

"I worry about you. All the time, I—"

"Shhhhhhh," she said.

There is a small Heinrich Böll story called "Parting." A crowded train station in Germany, in the chaotic aftermath of World War II. A soldier is seeing off a woman he will never see again, a woman he's known, as he puts it, for longer than there's been dirt and hunger. She's standing on the train already. He's below her on the platform. She's heading to be with her husband, a former prisoner of war who is now in Sweden lecturing on art history. "Parting" opens with a sentence I could repeat in my sleep:

> We were in that bleak, miserable mood that comes when you have already said goodbye but can't part because the train hasn't left yet.

At one point, the woman, Charlotte, says, Can you believe it, first the hair-raising escape, and now he's in Stockholm lecturing on Rubens? The soldier suddenly shouts, Oh, shut up! What, Charlotte asks, horrified. What? Forgive me, the soldier says, it's just my leg. I talk to it sometimes.

> The voice that always announces train departures sounded out now one platform closer, and I held my breath, but it was not our platform. The voice was only announcing the arrival of an international train from Rotterdam to Basel, and as I looked at Charlotte's small delicate face, I suddenly recalled the smell of soap and coffee, and I felt utterly wretched.

M handed me back the brownie. Our fingers touched briefly. I tried to say something. She put her finger to her lips. Enough. I sat there chewing the fucking brownie.

A half hour later, the man who'd let me in, a kind, shriveled man with a vague Eastern European accent—Polish? Czech?—came and told me it was time to leave. It was mandatory rest period, and the TV room was closing. M stayed on the bench and looked at her hands. The old Pole or Czech walked me out to the corridor, unlocked the doors, and let me out.

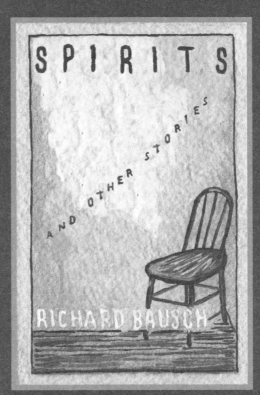

WHAT FEELS LIKE THE WORLD

The Garfield Pool at Twenty-sixth and Harrison, San Francisco. This morning I slip my six bucks through the little hole in the cage. Nobody's around, so I ring the little bell for service. I'm not much of a bell ringer. Some mornings I don't ring the bell at all, I just stand there and hope. But today, for some reason, I softly ping the bell with my knuckle. The guy comes out.

"It's eight forty-five."

"So?"

"Lap swim closes at nine on Wednesdays."

"Shit."

It's the older guy who's bald, not the older guy with the mop of hair, and he's got a whistle around his neck. He pushes my six bucks back through the hole.

"Keep that," he says. "Go take a swim."

Maybe it is the welcome darkness of this morning. I've been waiting so long for it to be gray. But it occurs to me as I do the few laps I've got time to do that if there's such a thing as pure beauty in this world (I'm still not entirely convinced, but let's just say), then it was right there in the bald old guy's "Keep that. Go take a swim."

The Garfield Pool is named for President James Garfield. Why? Who knows? All you need to know about the Garfield is: NO CHANGE GIVEN. Ten-dollar bill? Forget about it. It's been exact change at the Garfield Pool since President Garfield was shot in 1881. So many mornings I've found myself scrambling to come up with six dollars cash—in singles, quarters, nickels—that I can't emphasize enough how precious those six bucks are. I've got only eight or so minutes to swim, but it's a free eight minutes. I'm not an especially good swimmer. I avoid the fast lane and the pricks in Speedos. (The rest of us can't swim the butterfly, but why lord it over us and hog the lane?) So I'm bumbling along in the medium-fast lane thinking, Keep that, Keep that, and I get stuck on this idea of pure beauty existing or not existing in the world, and this reminds me of a story, because everything that happens to me reminds me, one way or another, of a story, in this case, Tobias Wolff's "Bullet in the Brain," that famous wallop of a story about a book-hating book critic who gets shot in the head during a bank robbery. As the bullet travels through his brain, the critic, in the nanoseconds he's got left, has a vision of possibly the single moment in his life when he just appreciated something for what it was. Not how it could be made better if some hack had the skills. For what it was, period. It's the memory of a kid playing baseball, one of the other boys saying, if I remember right, "Shortstop's the best position they is"—and this sentence, in particular the words "they is," has remained lodged in the critic's synapses. Two imperfect words, and yet they're human, and what this guy has been lacking for a long time now is any humanness whatsoever. The book critic dies with an image so moving his impermeable heart nearly bursts.

In the time I've got left in the pool, I try to think of other stories that have threatened to explode my own heart. It is August 2014. My father died four months ago and I remain numb not so much from shock as from not knowing what to think. So I don't think at all.

Instead, I summon another story, this one by Richard Bausch. I can't remember the name of it, but as I swim my final lap, I conjure up a grandfather watching his granddaughter jump rope in the morning rain. The granddaughter is heavy and she's been trying to lose weight to get ready for a gymnastics show where she must haul herself over a vaulting horse. As much as she practices, she can't do it. And as much as she diets, she can't lose weight. (This is America for you. Our fifth-graders diet.) And the day of the show is approaching. She's the only kid in her grade who can't get over the vaulting horse. And I'm swimming and I'm remembering being alone in the apartment and reading this story. My daughter wasn't born yet, but she was on the way (I'd seen her on a computer screen), and so this must have had something to do with it. I must have been intuiting the helplessness of fatherhood. I was so struck by this grandfather's love for his chubby granddaughter that I basically fell apart. I had to lie down on the floor and just breathe. I can't remember whether the daughter made it over the vaulting horse or not. I'm not sure it matters. All I've got to go on is this one scene where a grandfather watches his granddaughter jump rope in the rain, or try to jump rope, because she's not very good at it— and then the whistle blows—"Everybody out!"—and so I thank the old bald guy, get dressed, walk the two blocks home, and find the Bausch collection buried under a pile of books. In the park across the street, I reread the story.

It's called "What Feels Like the World." At first it sounds like a grandiose title, but when I finish it a second time, I understand why Bausch called it this. Weirdly, the story does feel like the world. What I mean is the story is about what it is like to be alive, and one way it is like to be alive is to stand by impotent, unable to protect the people we love from all the casual cruelties life offers. (Gym class being only one on a long list.) In this story, standing by is made a lot harder to take by the fact that the girl, Brenda, has recently lost her mother in a car accident and is now being raised by her widowed grandfather, a dumbfounded man if there ever was one. The grandfather is retired, but he thinks that if he gives the appearance of working every day, Brenda's home life will feel more stable. Each day, after he drops her off at school, the man pretends to be working at the bank. So he putters around his house all day; he can't clean it for fear that Brenda will figure out he no longer has a job.

The first time I read "What Feels Like the World" I felt intensely sorry for the little girl. Now, here in the park, I don't feel sorry for her at all. The kid's going to be all right. In spite of all the humiliations she will suffer at the hands of gym teachers who will never know what it's like to practice and practice and practice and still not be able to do something, she's going to be all right. Brenda's tough, a battler. It's the grandfather I worry about now. He's only in his sixties, but he won't be around forever, and he's got to live for the rest of his life knowing that one day she'll be on her own. And don't all parents, grandparents, face this? All our daughters—and all our sons—at some point will have to face this world without us.

How can I defend my own kid from people who might force her to do gymnastics if she doesn't want to (and this includes me)? But like I say, the kid is stronger. Maybe the kids will always be stronger. It's us—the impostors masquerading as protectors—who are unimaginably weak.

For a long time I thought reading would somehow make me a better writer. So I'd read in order to write. I'd justify the hours I spent with my feet up and call reading "my work." Now I see how ludicrous this is. All the Chekhov in thirteen volumes won't help me write a sentence that breathes. That comes from somewhere else, somewhere out in the world, where mothers die in car accidents and daughters hide the pain. And yet I have come to the conclusion that reading keeps me alive, period. I wake to read and sleep so I can get up in the morning and read some more. I haven't done much justice to "What Feels Like the World." There will always be more to say about how certain stories burrow into your brain and nonexistent people become ours for good. Brenda and her grandfather make my hold on my own flesh and blood seem all the more precarious.

I sit in Precita Park at the base of Bernal Hill and mourn a grandfather who's got years to live. I root for a motherless girl to get over an unnecessary leather hump. I think of my father and how tiny he looked in the hospital in Chicago. I kept thinking, Where did all the rest of him go? And I watch, sitting here motionless, what feels like the world, watch some people walk their dogs, others scurrying late to work, unlocking their cars with remote control. Bleep. Bleep. *Bleep.* At the corner of Precita and Harrison, a van pauses at the stop sign. It's filled with cleaning women. The van's windows are closed. The women are all staring straight ahead. They look exhausted already. It's only 10:00 a.m. And the mops standing up and pressed against the back window are like the other tired heads, only smaller.

VIRGIE WALKING AWAY

Or put it this way: If I could only be as brave in the face of defeat and death as Virgie Rainey in Welty's "The Wanderers."

(Only words on a page? Virgie?)

I think of her swimming in the Big Black River on the day of her mother's death. *She took off her clothes and let herself into the river.* I think of her swimming in the bright afternoon light. *Her breasts around which she felt the water curving were as sensitive at that moment as the tips of wings must feel to birds, or antennae to insects.* I think of her rising. *She stood and walked along the soft mud of the river bottom, and pulled herself out of the water by a willow branch which like a warm rain brushed her back with its leaves.* I think of the motionless little boys gaping at her as she disappears into the woods.

Because Virgie was the wild one, the unpredictable one, the one nobody could control. And yet, so gifted, too. A prodigy, a wunderkind. Miss Eckhart's star pupil. I think of how forcefully she played Franz Liszt's *Fantasy on Beethoven's Ruins of Athens*. When she was through, she was delirious and covered in enviable sweat...

And now look at her. Look who's ruined now. But even her failing fails. She's never fallen so low she can't get up again. Not that, even with all that God-given talent, anybody in Morgana had truly ever expected her to amount to anything. Virgie may have been a genius, but at heart, she was still white trash. Her father, Fate, sold buttermilk. Her mother, Katie, hawked ice cream. What do you expect from a family like that?

Still, people love a downfall.

Hardly able to hold down a job, and chronically incapable of keeping a man in spite of her always chasing one or another. *Remember that sailor Virgie ran after?* But what's it to her? Let Morgana talk.

Late on the night of her mother's funeral, there's a knock on the door. Virgie answers and finds a stranger holding a flower, a night-blooming cereus.

Virgie looked at the naked, luminous, complicated flower, large and pale as a face on the dark porch. . . .

"It's for you. Keep it—won't do the dead no good. And tomorrow, it'll look like a wrung chicken's neck. Look at it enduring the night.

And now she is leaving again. The last time she left Morgana she was seventeen. She swore she wouldn't come back, but she did. Endless the roads that bring us back home, endless the roads that carry us away again. Today Virgie's forty. She's no Huck Finn. Doesn't matter. This time, she tells herself, this time she'll be gone from here for good. As long as I'm conscious and able to think, I—whoever I am—will love Virgie Rainey as she walks away, in high heels, through the tall, bearded grass. Words on a page? Virgie? Virgie Rainey?

A.S. BYATT

BOOKER PRIZE-WINNING AUTHOR OF

POSSESSION AND BABEL TOWER

THE

MATISSÉ

STORIES

"Luminous"
— The New York Times Book Review

CINCINNATI, 2001

That year we lived on Erkenbrecher Avenue in an apartment in a crumbling Queen Ann with a bulbous tower above the third floor. I was always trying to find a way to break into the tower, but the door was bricked in. The place was down the block from the Cincinnati Zoo. In April, riots broke out in Over-the-Rhine after another routine killing of an unarmed black man by Cincinnati police. The city declared a curfew. For three nights, M broke it and rode her bike down Vine to McMicken Avenue to document the protests. One night a cop on a stallion nearly trampled her, but she was there, taking pictures. My version of civil disobedience was jogging, after curfew, up in genteel Clifton Gaslight.

Those leafy streets of red brick. Those old-timey streetlights fueled by real gas. On Ludlow Avenue, there was a place called Biagio's where we went for meatball soup. Biagio knew us by name. *You two deadbeats again? Can't either of you cook?* I think of his laugh, a true belly laugh. There should be more to remember. Why isn't there more to remember?

There was a couch in the kitchen (there was no living room, only a bedroom and kitchen), and I remember lying there during the riots and listening to the elephants and waiting for M to come home. Sometimes the elephants would screech, other times they'd moan. The moaning was worse. We had an upstairs neighbor, a small girl with spiky hair. She'd sit outside on her stoop in front of the house and read. I remember one of the books was a copy of *The Matisse Stories* by A. S. Byatt, which has a beautiful light blue cover. On it two people are reading. There's a window and tree in the background. This neighbor and M became friends that year, and they'd sometimes sit out there on the stoop and talk in low voices. It was all very serious. A brief, serious, now vanished friendship. I'd spy on them and try and listen to what they were saying by hiding beneath an open window in our apartment. I've forgotten her name, the Matisse girl. I remember wanting to smell her shoulders.

Where's she now? Where are we?

Our landlord was a retired geography professor at the University of Cincinnati. If we were late with the rent, he politely docked us five dollars. He'd accompany the receipt for the five dollars with a note asking us to "mind" the calendar. He'd also, depending on the season, leave us tomatoes from his garden in our mailbox.

I was teaching at Miami of Ohio. We'd lasted five days in Oxford, a town, it seemed to us, made up almost entirely of fraternities, and ended up fleeing to Cincinnati as if it were the promised land. M got a job as a producer at the public-access TV station, a job she loved. The motto of the station was: "To everyone their own show." What happened to cable-access television? Is there still such a thing? One of M's shows starred a woman who recited the Bible while she did aerobics. *I have come to bring not peace but a sword!*

Now lift those buns, lift, lift, lift. And in Over-the-Rhine, the cops shot another man—kid? It depended on who was talking about it. The city burned. M rode her bike down there with her camera. When she took pictures—this I refuse to forget—M always put one eye to the lens and pulled her other eye closed with her fingers.

DUSK

AND OTHER STORIES

JAMES
SALTER

SALTER

Dusk in the city, the traffic, the buses pouring light, reflections in windows, optician's shops.

—James Salter

He found such beauty in our inability to live up to our lives. This alone, the infinite ways we screw up the finite years we're granted, might have kept James Salter alive a few more years. People keep dying. There's nothing profound in this, but I think of Dante, standing on the edge of hell, surprised by the sheer numbers: *I hadn't thought death had undone so many.*

Salter's obituary in *The New York Times* focused, at length, on how unfamous he was. As if fame is the sole basis by which we judge a lifetime of work. When will we cut this shit out? And enough with the writer's writer stuff. He wrote for readers, if not for millions, then for enough of them.

Not everything he did was perfect, or even close. I remember once being so irritated by a lush sentence in *Light Years* that I threw the book across the room. I let it lie there, sprawled, languid, portentous, for a few minutes before diving across the carpet for it. I couldn't go on reading, I had to go on reading. That's the sort of writer Salter is. He reels you in. He repels you. He reels you in.

It's ten after seven. My daughter's asleep. It's just me and the kid. Her mom's already on her way to work. I've spent the last hour searching this garage in vain for Salter's *Dusk and Other Stories*. Got to be here somewhere. The simple act of looking for it has been enough to bring back the way his stories leave me simultaneously elated and bereft. I don't need the book; I only need the notion of the book.

In fewer than ten pages, Salter can cut so deep into the desperate clench of a marriage he'll make you wonder if he's been hiding out under your bed.

And it isn't the sentences. Reviewers have always done flips over Salter's sentences, especially in novels like *A Sport and a Pastime*. Oh, that James Salter, my God, those gorgeous sentences. I've always taken this to be a backhanded way of suggesting that the whole package didn't quite measure up to the glory of the individual sentences. Yet in the stories, as opposed to the novels, the sentences are far more compact and, mercifully, less noticeable. In the stories, character, not language, is paramount. In the stories, there is never any unnecessary lush. In the stories, Salter, like Isaac Babel (whom he loved), usually knew where to jab the period for maximum emotional devastation.

Dusk remains lost under some pile. I did manage to find *All That Is*, his baggy final novel, a book filled with much Salterian brilliance, the sentences, the sentences, as well as some of the schmaltzy male gaze Salter couldn't seem to edit out. Even a majestic sentence maker like James Salter, at times, in the face of beauty, is unable to say what he means to say. So he compensated by saying more than necessary. But don't we all?

Since it is all I have this morning, the house still quiet, I quote a paragraph from the end of *All That Is*. The point of view is that of a flawed man on the edge of death, contemplating all the singular memories that will vanish from the earth when he's gone:

> He would be going where they all had gone and—it was diffi-
> cult to believe—all he had known would go with him, the war,
> Mr. Kindrigen and the butler pouring coffee, London those
> first days, the lunch with Christine, her gorgeous body like
> a separate entity, names, houses, the sea, all he had known
> and things he had never known but were there nevertheless,
> things of his time, all the years, the great liners with their
> invincible glamour readying to sail, the band playing as they
> were backed away, the green water widening, the *Matsonia*
> leaving Honolulu, the *Bremen* departing, the *Aquitania*, *Ile de
> France*, and the small boats, following behind. The first voice
> he ever knew, his mother's, was beyond memory, but he could
> recall the bliss of being close to her as a child . . . life beyond
> reckoning, the life that had been opened to him and that he
> owned.

Right, lush in spots. In a story Salter wouldn't have allowed this paragraph to stand. Unlike Babel, Salter did live long enough to write badly. But for now, his stories still missing somewhere in this cold morning garage, I'll love what I've got, even *her gorgeous body like a separate entity*, and I'll sit here and think of my own mother's voice, and with my own daughter now bellowing from above at the top of her lungs, I'll squeeze in a little agnostic's prayer for James

Salter. A writer. An ex–Jewish fighter pilot who changed his name from Horowitz to sound less Jewish. A man who knew the hurt we inflict on one another and found a way to adore us anyway. And who understood that love, like time, has physical weight and that sometimes we can't carry either anymore.

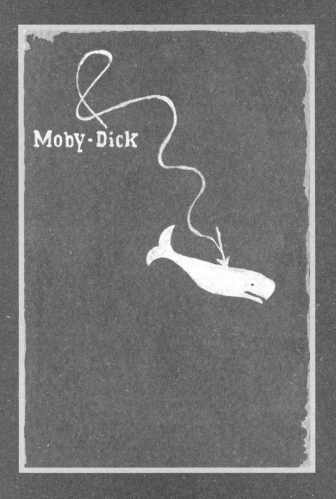

Moby-Dick

EARLY MORNING THOUGHTS ON AHAB

Last night, deep into *Moby-Dick*, on page 667 I was surprised when Ishmael announces, out of nowhere, that not very long before the *Pequod* set sail, Ahab was found, writhing in pain, on a cobblestone street in Nantucket. His ivory leg had buckled and stabbed him in the groin. This incident is the single glimpse in the entire novel of Ahab on land. Where was Ahab coming from? Was he on his way home? Ishmael doesn't seem to know. He doesn't even tell us how he knows this story or from whom he heard it. But he does say, curiously, that Ahab was found and assisted by "someone unknown." Imagine it. Ahab sprawled in the road, and a stranger comes to him, hoists him up—touches him. This strikes me. That this someone unknown would have had to touch Ahab's body in order to help him.

Ishmael claims that this accident so scarred Ahab that it explains why he remained locked in his cabin, seen by nobody, during the first few days of the voyage. At that time, hundreds of pages earlier in the book, Ishmael had remarked that he was nervous about Ahab's absence from the deck. A sailor likes to have an opportunity to size up his captain before entrusting the man with his life for three years. But by that time the *Pequod* was already under way, so what choice did he have?

When he does glimpse Ahab for the first time, Ishmael reports, the man looks like he's just been cut away from a burning stake.

Now here comes Ishmael's assertion, again seriously late in the game, if you ask me, that Ahab's demented state of mind stems as much from this falling in the street as the white whale's munching his leg off in the first place.

This all got me thinking this morning. I was standing by the edge of the cliff at the end of Poplar Road in Bolinas. Below my feet, Ahab's last ocean. On the shoreline, the waves played with some logs as if they were chopsticks.

> "Ahoy there! This is the *Pequod*, bound round the world! Tell them to address all future letters to the Pacific Ocean! and this time three years, if I am not at home, tell them to—"

Tell them to what? Ahab never finishes this line, shouted to the ghost ship *Goney*, bound for home.

I find that lately I do more reading than writing, and more thinking, by far, than either. I read at night until I fall asleep with the light on, some book tented over my nose, and in the morning I wander around the edge of this cliff thinking about what I read the night before. But isn't thinking a form of writing without the pressure of needing to communicate with anybody? I'm testing out the possibility of writing a book in my head without pen, paper, or computer. The Israeli novelist Yoel Hoffmann once wrote: "It did once indeed occur to this author that he could write a book that is all blank pages."

It is July 2015. A terrible month in America is over. In Charleston, just a few weeks ago, less than a mile away from where my daughter's grandmother lives, a boy with a similar bowl haircut to the one I had as a kid spent an hour listening to a group of people talk about the Bible. That night the group was studying the gospel of St. Mark. Jesus delivers a sermon from out on a boat to accommodate the huge crowd that has gathered on the shore to hear him. He tells the parable of the sower and compares the likelihood of seed thriving in different places to degrees of receptivity among the faithful to the message of the gospel. It all depends on how people listen.

> And these are they which are sown on good ground, such as hear the Word and receive it and bring forth fruit: some thirtyfold, some sixty, and some a hundred.

I ask this honestly, not rhetorically: Did that kid hear a word of any of it? Did a single word penetrate?

If you're not home in three years, tell them to what, Ahab? Did you know even then that you'd never come home again?

Maybe he was just afraid. Like so many people are afraid. Maybe this is all it ever amounted to, ordinary fear. Ahab was afraid to stay home, afraid to walk his own streets. Afraid, for some reason, to go home to his family, to his own wife and young son. Afraid, so he had no choice but to sail on. But there is a moment, just before all hell breaks loose, when Starbuck tries to convince him to believe in something beyond himself. He implores Ahab to turn the boat eastward. It's not too late to change direction and call this voyage quits. The two of them could still live to see their wives and children again.

> "Oh, my Captain! my Captain! noble soul! grand old heart, after all! why should any one give chase to that hated fish! Away with me! let us fly these deadly waters! let us home. Wife and child, too, are Starbuck's—wife and child of his brotherly, sisterly play-fellow youth; even as thine, sir, are the wife and child of thy loving, paternal old age! Away! let us away!—this instant let me alter the course! How cheerily, how hilariously, O my Captain, would we bowl on our way to see old Nantucket again! I think, Sir, they have some such mild blue days, even as this, in Nantucket."

Let us home. There's no sadder sentence in *Moby-Dick*. And by God, it nearly works. Ahab responds:

> "They have, they have. I have seen them—some summer days in the morning. About this time—yes, it is his noon nap now—the boy vivaciously wakes; sits up in bed; and his mother tells him of me, of cannibal old me; how I am abroad upon the deep, but will yet come back to dance him again."

Of course, if they'd given up the hunt, we wouldn't have a tragedy, and without a tragedy we wouldn't have the book. Plot's got to do what plot's got to do. But maybe this is why I've always been so wary of it. It forces characters to do something, anything, when all they should be doing is heading home.

But did you notice something? Ahab, of all people on earth, knows the exact time of day his kid wakes up from his nap. Daddy

Ahab! Ahab never will get back to dance that boy again and he knows it. Maybe Ahab concocted the whole insane, murderous ordeal to simply avoid having to go home. Because there, and only there, existed a nameless terror he couldn't sail onward into the deep and pretend to hunt.

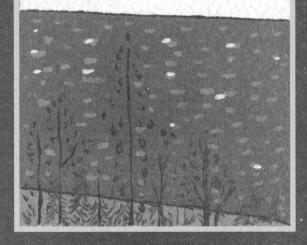

LOVE
AND
SHAME
AND
LOVE

ALL FATHERS ARE FICTIONAL

In the end, he took up so little space. This is what I still can't seem to get over. He'd never been large, but he'd always had a thick, bearlike solidity. My father was the sort of man who looked natural blocking a doorway. It seemed an overly cruel joke to take away what little was left of his body. He wasn't asking much by then. In fact, he wasn't asking anything at all. Just a McDonald's milkshake once a day, and my father didn't even ask for that, we just knew he liked it. He'd fumble for the cup with both his hands, take a few sips, and fall back asleep with the striped straw in his mouth. My father's teeth. He'd always taken such good care of them. What happened to my father's teeth?

I've had my share of father figures. When Andre Dubus died in 1999, I cried my eyes raw, and I remember standing in line at the wake and reaching for his oldest son, Andre, who pulled me close and whispered, "We just have to walk through the hole he made." I've clung to those words for a long time. But my old, gone friend would have been the first to say: *Easier to be a figure than a father.*

* * *

A LaSalle Street lawyer for almost fifty years, when he retired I'm not sure my father even knew who he was anymore. After so many years of hustling—he said the only way to accomplish anything in this world is to hustle, and when you're done hustling, start hustling—his whole being seemed to instantaneously retreat. For the first time in his life he began watching television. In the beginning, I was relieved. I thought he might at last turn into a normal American. But TV became a substitute for everything. He'd watch cable news endlessly, as if the frantic agitation in those voices brought him a little closer to the way things used to be at the office.

In fiction, characters roughly based on my father haven't had it easy. I've exposed family laundry that, with the revisionist morality of hindsight, I now regret. I will say this, though: My father never gave me any grief about my work, because he was a charitable reader who understood the difference between nonfiction that tries to tell the truth and fiction that uses some truth to find something else. For me writing has always been about holding up a mirror to life and then smashing it on the floor. I pick up a random piece and stare at it for days. Out of this: stories. My father understood this, too. I think he knew that the fictional person he resembled was only some rescued fragment.

But the fact is, my father was someone that people often referred to as "a real character." When I was growing up and still lived in his house, my friends used to come over just to listen to him growl. The problem was being actually related to him. His rants were terrific comedy, if they weren't thundering at you. My father had strange fastidious ways. When anything or anybody failed to meet his highest standards, he'd detonate. At home, at work, or on the street. For some reason vacations were the scenes of my father's epically worst behavior. There are hotel staffs from Rome to Tokyo who still have nightmares involving a certain irate little man in a bow tie. All my life I wished my father was like other dads. Now Eric and I (and our younger sister, Rebecca, and brother, Will) shrug off the rage, and even miss it. Just after the funeral, after we'd poured three shovelfuls of dirt each over the urn that contained my father's ashes, Will said, "Damn, for months, I just wished he'd start yelling about something, anything."

In a novel called *Love and Shame and Love*, I killed off a father at the Brooks Brothers on Michigan Avenue. I have vivid memories of shopping there with my father. When I was little, he dressed me in sailor suits. He would say, "Look at the little admiral. A tiny Rickover, a miniature Lord Nelson." To this day, I can't stomach the navy, anybody's navy. When I got older and it was time for me to wear ties, he'd noose them so tight around on my neck I could hardly breathe. This was all part of becoming a man in the city of Chicago. And yet my Brooks Brothers heart-attack scene was written less out of revenge than warped affection. I wanted my character, the loop lawyer Philip Popper, to die in a place that felt comfortable.

Philip roams Brooks Brothers like a leopard in his own jungle. This particular hue of blue all his. Today, though, he's not on the prowl.

He's come in for—

What has he come in for? . . .

The salesman looks for a moment at Philip's cordovans, then back at Philip's face, as if he's begun to understand. His eyes moisten slightly. *There is comfort in our blueality. I know it. You know it. Nothing to be ashamed of. Here the harshness of the world is lessened.*

It's bad form to laugh at your own stuff; worse, infinitely worse, going-to-hell worse, when the subject is the last moments of a character inspired by your father. Yet by the end of the scene, as its point of view shifts, I wasn't laughing anymore. The pain in Philip's chest is getting slowly sharper. He's begun to lose his balance. He's begun to realize what is happening.

> This is all very off. We stumble from late fall to early winter. Where did that come from? Did I read it somewhere? Dizzier now, discombobulated. Brooks Brothers afternoon. Outside, the steam rises from the vents in the sidewalk, the underground boilers, a burbling cauldron beneath these streets. In here a sinkingness, a muffled feeling, not at all unpleasant. The salesman might be saying something else, but his voice is so far away now.

As I've said, my father was a charitable reader, and he always read with a sense of humor. After finishing the book, he called and said the book wasn't too bad but—"You know, Brooks isn't what it used to be. Now the bastards make all their suits in Taiwan."

You'd think that since I spent so much time choreographing a version of my father's death, I'd be prepared for it when it actually happened. Never has fiction seemed so useless. The other morning, over a box of doughnut holes, I talked to a friend about this.

"I'm confused."

"Not uncommon."

"All the years I spent not calling him back. He'd call and he'd call. My kid was born and I didn't call him back for a week. Now I'm lonely?"

"Does that mean you aren't mourning?"

I popped a doughnut hole. "Wait, I'm sad?"

"That's my diagnosis."

"He cut us out of the will, didn't leave me or Eric a dime. Not that I begrudge my—"

"Does this all mean you aren't sad?"

"Not a hundred bucks, not his watch. Not even one of his shotguns. Nada, nada, nada."

My father was reduced to soot before I even made it back to Chicago. The April day we buried the tiny box (half the size of a shoe box), it snowed. Call it late, late winter. His name was Ronald A. Orner. When he was born, my grandparents apparently forgot to give him a middle name. When he opened his own law practice in 1962, my father bestowed on himself a noble middle initial. A young attorney on the make trying to increase his gravitas. The last time I saw him I kissed his sunken, unshaved cheek as he slept.

RONALD A. ORNER

Ronald A. Orner, born November 25, 1935, to the late Seymour and Lorraine (Spinner) Orner, passed away peacefully April 10, 2014, in Highland Park, Illinois, his lifelong home. Ronald was a 1953 graduate of Highland Park High School, attended the University of Wisconsin, and graduated from Northwestern Law School in 1958. He was a veteran of the U.S. Air Force. Orner was a prominent attorney in private practice for forty-nine years at Orner and Wasserman, the law firm he co-founded in 1962, and a member of the Chicago Bar Association. Active in civic and Democratic Party affairs, he helped build the modern Democratic Party in Lake County, which had been an Illinois Republican stronghold since the time of the Civil War. Orner was a losing candidate for the Illinois State Senate in 1970 and served as chairman of the Lake County Democratic Party. He was also a member of the Finance Committee of the Democratic National Committee under the chairmanship of Robert S. Strauss. He was a major fund-raiser for former Chicago mayor Jane M. Byrne. Ronald Orner was an avid hunter at the Richmond Hunt Club and a sailor at Wilmette Harbor. He was also a longtime member of the Standard Club of Chicago. Brother of the late Jacqueline Putterman, Ronald leaves his wife, Michelle (Mitzi); his children, Eric (Blake), Peter (Katherine), Rebecca, and William; and a granddaughter, Phoebe.

One other thing: Whenever my father was asked his name, he'd say it once and then spell it out. "Ronald Orner. O-R-N-E-R." I am my father's son. Whenever I say my name, I always, before I can even help myself, spell out the letters.

• • •

A FRANÇOIS MAURIAC
50¢ WINNER OF THE NOBEL PRIZE FOR LITERATURE
0-5181

LIFE OF JESUS

LETTER FROM NEW MELLERAY, IOWA

You know that moment of resignation when you know you're just about to get hit in the face? Well, you wouldn't. You're five. In any case, you will. I wish I could protect you from it. I'm sorry to have to tell you this. I've been approaching life lately with this useless too-late flinch on my face, waiting for an inevitable punch. After you and your beautiful red-haired mother left for South Carolina last week, I've been in a daze. Tired but sleepless. At night I tried running up and down the stairs to make some noise, but it was never enough. Getting high didn't help, either. Why am I telling you all this? Lately, when I've been talking to myself, I imagine that there's one person who can hear me, and that's you. It's a burden, I know, but that's what you get for being born. You have to listen to your parents try to explain things they have no business explaining like when you asked the other day why girls and boys have different parts and I said it had to do with the diet of monkeys back when they were transitioning into humans. I'm not sure this was an accurate answer. We fill the silence, don't we? But there is a silence that is much louder than silence. I hope you never hear it, or at least, when you do, that it is by choice.

I decided a change of scenery might help lift my mood a little, and get me away from the space you two left behind. I left the dog with Rosie. I arrived here yesterday. Brother Francis sat me in his office and handed me the following schedule:

> Vigils: 3:30 a.m.
> Lauds: 6:30
> Mass: 7:00
> Reading/Private Prayer: 8:00
> Terce: 9:15
> Work: 9:30
> Sext: 11:45
> Lunch: 12:00 p.m.
> None: 1:45
> Work: 2:00
> Reading/Private Prayer: 4:30
> Vespers: 5:30
> Reading/Private Prayer: 6:00
> Supper: 7:00

"Everything's optional," Brother Francis said, "though we do invite all visiting meditants to evening vespers. No pressure. Also, if you're going to skip a meal, let me know and I'll inform the cook."

"Everything's optional?"

"For you. Not for us."

"What's Sext?"

"It's when we read the psalms."

"Oh. So I don't have to do anything at all? Nothing?"

"You sound disappointed."

"I was hoping—" What was I hoping? "I seek discipline," I said. "And some sort of spiritual enlightenment that isn't, you know, too religious. But I'm open. At least to a degree. Also, I'd like to stop living in the past. And if I could be less materialistic and shallow, that would be terrific."

Brother Francis looked at his watch. He's a kind man, used to agitated souls wandering in here day after day, but he's also busy as hell.

"I'm Jewish," I said.

"Last week we had a tour bus full of Hindus. The week before that, a dozen atheists from Texas." Brother Francis threw me a bone: "We lock the door at ten."

"Awesome."

"But if you should find yourself locked out, you can always ring the bell outside the front door and the night porter will—"

I didn't last long not being locked up. I had to at least *pretend* to escape. So this morning, after Lauds, I snuck out and set off for Dubuque to get a cup of coffee. Nothing against the coffee here at the abbey. It's actually pretty good. There's a coffee room where you can get it 24/7. Just like at a Comfort Inn. Even so, I had to run from something. This, too, I hope you learn only on your own terms. It is spring in eastern Iowa and the fields are green, jungle green, the sort of carpet green that makes you want to roll around out there with a farmer's wife. Perhaps this is an inappropriate thing to say.

In Dubuque, looking for the Starbucks, I drove down Grandview Avenue, where the bright yellow recycling boxes gleamed in the driveways of house after house. I tried to have a spiritual experience over those recycling boxes. It nearly worked. You should have seen them. The people of Dubuque never forget to put out the recycling, and they always sort it very well, too.

The underlying lie here is that I've come to this place to finish a book I may never finish. In the meantime, I've spent my days walking the abbey grounds and watching other people work very hard. At the moment, it is Reading/Private Prayer (third round) and I'm sitting in the monastery library. A monk nearby is reading the latest issue of *The New York Review of Books*. I wish I were making this up. Myself, I tried to get in the spirit and browsed the shelves. I pulled off François Mauriac's *Life of Jesus* and began reading. It's pretty good so far, though I keep putting the book down to think about you. Mauriac says that the Bible says nothing at all about those years that a carpenter, son of Mary and Joseph, lived in the village of Nazareth, of which there was no mention in history and which the Old Testament does not name.

> There he lived for thirty years—but not in a silence of ado-
> ration and love. Jesus dwelt in the thick of a clan, in the
> midst of the petty talk, the jealousies, the small dramas of
> numerous kin.

Petty talk and jealousy don't sound too bad compared to being hammered to a couple of pieces of lumber. Let's hear it for small dramas. Send a little my way, Jesus. But back then he wasn't the Son of God, either. No, wait, he was the Son of God even then, it's just that nobody knew it. *Did he know it?* Or did he just have a nagging intuition that there might be some new career opportunities on the horizon? Mauriac also says Jesus was one of three carpenters in Nazareth and he wasn't even considered the best. Maybe he felt he had to branch out into another line of work. Make his mark another way. Who wants to be a second-fiddle carpenter in a town of three carpenters? So—he started making miracles, and that was the beginning of it. Or the end of it, depending on how you look at it.

But before all that, Mauriac imagines what Jesus and Mary might have talked about all those years over the dinner table after Joseph died. Poor Joseph, poor unfather who even so *was* a father. So that when he was gone, Jesus was fatherless, at least on earth. And there was Mary, a single mother, sitting with the future King of the World, "whose reign shall have no end," and apparently she knew it all along.

But Mauriac says there must have been times over the years when even she—his mother—must have questioned the prophecy. But if she did, she kept her doubts to herself. And as parents, we do always hope for the best for our children, whatever their endeavors. For the record, I want you to know that your mother and I will support whatever you feel you want to be, including, if you're so inclined, mankind's savior. In any case, Mauriac conjectures that Jesus and Mary must have talked a lot about tools. I like that. This seems as good an answer as any. When in doubt about the future, talk about tools.

Love, your only father

Yasunari Kawabata

Palm-of-the-Hand Stories

A PALM-OF-THE-HAND STORY

Not long before his suicide in April 1972, Yasunari Kawabata did something that has perplexed me for years. I'm still not sure what to make of it, and I only mention it because it's been on my mind this morning. Something about this morning's sun after last night's hard rain. I was up much of the night listening to the wind pierce the cracks in the cabin walls. A four-hundred-year-old redwood went down in front of the McRaes'. Even the dog was terrified and hid in the closet. I woke up groggy and murderous for coffee (finding none), went outside, and there it was: the pale sun through the wet branches. There was no wind and I listened to the ceaseless churn of the ocean. Another morning, the light through the trees.

And I remembered this odd fact I once read about Kawabata: how three months before his death he took one of his most loved novels, *Snow Country,* and rewrote it, by hand, into a brief story, what Kawabata called a "palm-of-the hand story."

Kawabata began *Snow Country* in 1934 and finished it in 1947. The story, "Gleanings from Snow Country," was published posthumously in the fall of 1972. It is safe to say that this particular story preoccupied him for much of his writing life. You could make an argument that by reworking an old story, especially one that had brought him such acclaim, Kawabata may have been trying to bask again in former glory. But beyond this, isn't there just something about our own past words that is comforting? Did I actually write that? Think that? Was I once so perceptive? Have you experienced this? When the you who wrote certain words, or did certain things, is so long gone you don't recognize yourself? This morning I wonder if something else wasn't motivating Kawabata to return to the same terrain. Maybe he felt he wasn't quite finished. I think he may have suspected there was more to be found there, one more wrenching layer to the story of the two doomed lovers amid the snow and mountains.

When I think of the novel now I don't think of the flames that eventually engulf the story. As must be clear by now, I'm not a reader who needs a lot of drama. Life is enough of a roller coaster as it is. No, I want to lift my eyes from the page and see something familiar in a different light. I want to have visions. I think of reading *Snow Country* and I remember how the book brought me home to the Chicago cold, and how when I was a kid I used to lie facedown in the snow, for as long as I could, to try to freeze my eyelids shut.

The story, like the novel, opens with a scene on a train. A man, Shimamura, takes his finger and wipes the condensation off the window so he can see out. He is shocked by an eye staring directly at him, superimposed on the desolate landscape rolling by. It's only a reflection of the eye of the girl sitting across from him, a fellow passenger, but at first, for those couple of moments, Shimamura is completely discombobulated as together the snow country and the eye move across his vision like "a double-exposed motion picture." It's the sort of moment when fiction crosses a border and, reading itself, transcends words on page and becomes lived experience. Like Shimamura, we can't separate the strange floating eye from "the waves of night darkness" beyond the window.

By compressing an already aching, hallucinatory novel into an eleven-page story, Kawabata may have been trying to isolate only what he may have considered most essential, such as this specter of an eye in the window. But "Gleanings" is not a greatest hits of *Snow Country*; if it were, it would fail. Kawabata doesn't simply condense the book by doing away with the scaffolding that holds it up as a novel. Instead, he does something more radical. Kawabata chooses exclusively scenes that are from the beginning of the novel in an effort, I believe, to create a new and wholly independent story that is suggestive rather than conclusive.

In "Gleanings from Snow Country" we know little about Shimamura. He's simply a man returning by train to a small village in the mountains in order to reunite with a woman. This woman, unlike in *Snow Country*, where she is called Komako, remains nameless in the story. And love itself, in the story, is doomed less by external circumstances, by facts, than by some inexpressible fate. In the novel, it's clear that Shimamura must eventually go home again to his family in Tokyo. In the story, there is no family, and the two lovers are haunted by the mere sound of the steam whistle of the midnight train to Tokyo, as it drifts up to them from the valley below.

"Close the window."
"Stay like this a little longer."

Kawabata must have no longer felt the need to worry over the machinations of plot, to provide context or backstory. And when you think about it, what's plot or context or backstory compared to the ultimate story, the emptiness that was settling in on the writer himself?

* * *

In *Snow Country*, there is a division of time between the present action and what the lovers call "then," those few days just after they met for the first time, exactly 199 days earlier. She's been counting. In the story, there is no "then" time. "Then" and now are compressed and occur nearly simultaneously. Maybe this is why Komako goes unnamed in this later incarnation? Because Kawabata sought to recapture that lost time before Shimamura's lust bled into love? What I mean is he rolls back *what happens* and returns to a time when anything is possible.

> She sullenly hung her head, and Shimamura could see down the nape of her neck that even her back had turned red, as though a fresh, wet nakedness had been exposed.

Sex—how could I leave this out? Because there isn't any, at least not any on the page. And yet every line of "Gleanings" is infused with a hardly containable sexual charge. Nothing remotely romantic about any of it. Shimamura is a shallow cad from Tokyo up in the mountains looking for a reprise of their fling. At least at first. Still, through some inexplicable alchemy, this doesn't make the reunion of these two any less intense.

> His hand was inside the neck of her kimono.
> She did not respond to his request. The woman folded her arms to bar the way to what Shimamura sought, but, numb with drunkenness, she had no strength.
> "What's this? Damn you. Damn you. It won't move—this arm!" She suddenly put her head down on her own arm.
> Startled, he let go. There were deep tooth marks on her arm.

Why does the woman bite her own arm? And why in eleven pages do these tooth marks loom so much more forcefully than they do in *Snow Country*?

There amid the snow and the mountains, all the dark mountains, mountains beyond mountains, bright with snow, these two hold each other.

Was the sun about to rise? The brilliance of the snow in the mirror increased as if it were burning cold. And with it the purple-black luster of the woman's hair in the mirror grew deeper.

But it's not the snow itself. It is the snow in the mirror that makes it look as though it is burning. The same is true for the eye on the train. The reflection of a thing, not the thing itself, has become the source of all mystery. And so: the desperation connecting these two, as Shimamura studies her in the mirror, becomes—how is it possible?—even more extreme. What Kawabata seems to have been after, and what occupied his last days, was to feel, one last time, the ecstasy of a beginning.

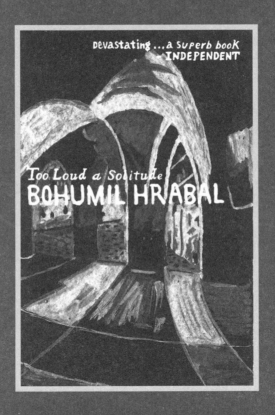

devastating ... a superb book
—INDEPENDENT

Too Loud a Solitude
BOHUMIL HRABAL

NIGHT TRAIN TO SPLIT

In 1999 M and I took an overnight train to Split, Croatia. On the train was a large group of drunken Russians who partied until dawn. A conductor told us, "Don't be fooled, those aren't Russians, they're Slovenes." The rowdiest of them all, by far, the conductor said, are the Slovenes. They're the ones who started all the trouble in Yugoslavia in the first place.

I must have been reading something on that trip. It might well have been *Too Loud a Solitude*. I remember giving up on Milan Kundera after discovering the crowded loneliness of Bohumil Hrabal. Czechs say the writer is so idiosyncratic as to be untranslatable. I'll take what I can get. Because an approximation of the "real" Hrabal has been, for a long time, more than enough for me. That year I read *Too Loud a Solitude* compulsively, and still keep it close in order to disappear again into the loopy cadence of his prose and that gone time when M and I were other people who went by the same names. Prague in 1999. We were poor and young and stupid and happy. Let it stand without qualification. The first time I finished *Too Loud a Solitude*, I was up in Letná Park, and I remember leaping off the bench and running around in circles, holding the book above my head and shouting because I believed I'd experienced some religious illumination. A brief, ninety-eight-page, lightning strike of a novel, the book is about a man named Hanta who has been crushing paper beneath a street in Prague for the last thirty-five years. People throw paper and books, books by the barrelful, down Hanta's hole in the pavement. Before he crushes them, Hanta reads. The book of Ecclesiastes, the Talmud, Goethe, Schiller, Nietzsche, Immanuel Kant's *Theory of the Heavens*. Kant, who argues that the heavens are not humane, nor is life above or below.

The most precious books he carries home with him. Hanta's little apartment is wall-to-wall packed with the books he's been hoarding for thirty-five years.

> Even the bathroom has only room enough for me to sit down in: just above the toilet bowl, about five feet off the floor, I have a whole series of shelves, planks piled high to the ceiling, holding over a thousand pounds of books, and one careless roost, one careless rise, one brush with a shelf, and half a ton of books would come tumbling down on me, catching me with my pants down.

Many of the books Hanta reads are either banned or strongly disapproved by the government, and *Too Loud a Solitude*, which was self-published in a *samizdat* edition in 1976 and didn't officially appear until the Velvet Revolution in 1989, is anti-Communist without lifting much of a finger. The book goes far beyond the politics of its time. Its relevance to today is unmistakable. *Too Loud a Solitude* is an elegy for the death of reading. It is also about how worship of unfettered technological progress invariably results in a trouncing of the human spirit. And it is about how only individual human memory has the unique power to redeem us. Hrabal would howl at all this grandiosity.

So I should add that, among other things, the book also has a healthy amount of human turds. Because no serious book that I know of takes itself less seriously than this one. Hanta is lustful and brainy and spends much of the book drunk as a lord. Down in his cellar beneath the street, Hanta talks to Jesus. He converses with Lao-tze. And he reads and he reads. He reads drunk, he reads sober. He reads the books he refuses to destroy and, through reading, recalls his life, his lost loves, his favorite uncle, and some famous turds the size of paperweights. He remembers the time he was mugged at knifepoint. But the guy wasn't after his wallet. What he wanted was someone— anyone—for once to listen to his poetry.

And Hanta remembers the lips of his Gypsy girlfriend, who disappeared during the war after being taken away by the Gestapo and sent to a concentration camp.

One evening I came home to find her gone.

Early in the book Hanta quotes the Talmud: "For we are like olives: only when we are crushed do we yield what is best in us." By the end of the novel, this line, devastatingly, is no longer a metaphor, and yet it wouldn't be an exaggeration to say that *Too Loud a Solitude* has rescued me from myself more than once. And there have been many times when I've wanted to mug people just to force them to take the book home and read it, slowly, letting each sentence echo in the brain. Call it the novel of my life, the one book, above all the others, that so entangles hope with despair that you can't tell one from the other. There's hope in this alone.

I can be by myself because I'm never lonely; I'm simply alone, living in my heavily populated solitude, a harum-scarum of infinity and eternity, and Infinity and Eternity seem to take a liking to me.

* * *

In 2015 I went back to Prague for a couple of days. I happened to be in Germany and so took a train from Munich. I'm not sure what I was looking for, but I went wandering in the neighborhood M and I had lived in sixteen years earlier, Vršovice off tramline 22. It took me an hour to find that first apartment—hard for me to believe, given how well my feet once knew the route from the tram stop to our door. How do we forget such things? When I finally found Kozacka 21, our landlord's name was still on a piece of ragged tape next to the buzzer. I could have sworn it was the same piece of tape as when we'd lived there. It seemed like a completely unnecessary miracle. I pressed the button and waited. Nobody answered. I pressed it again. Nothing. I unpeeled the piece of tape—DRAPOL—and slipped it into my pocket.

M is doing okay now. She's back in the Midwest, living near her family, working again in film, and writing. She's also doing her best to help other people with similar struggles at a local organization that is constantly under threat of being defunded. Hrabal says the heavens may not be humane, but this doesn't mean that, sometimes, not all the time, there isn't compassion and love down here on earth.

I remember waking up at dawn to the rocking of the train. The Slovenes had finally knocked off. We must have been south of Trieste by then. M was still asleep in the upper bunk. The light hadn't reached her face yet. I climbed the ladder and watched her breathe.

Outside, the fog was so thick it wasn't fog exactly, more like a curtain of rain that wasn't falling.

ELIAS
CANETTI

THE TONGUE SET FREE

PICADOR

FATHER'S DEATH: THE FINAL VERSION

Last night, at Pancho Villa on Sixteenth, I watched a woman tie and retie her shoelaces, over and over. She was alone at a little table. I was waiting for her to vacate, because I was also alone and wanted the little table for myself. The taqueria was jammed. There were no empty tables. The Giants had just lost Game 6 of the World Series. When teams win, people only want to get wasted; losing makes a whole city hungry. I stood there, burrito on my red plastic tray, and watched this woman tie and retie her left shoe. Just when she might have been satisfied, she leaned down again and undid the laces. I continued to hover. She was clearly finished eating. Whatever remained of her food was neatly tied up in a plastic bag and sitting before her on the table. Time's up, lady, I got a *carnitas especial* burning a hole in my tray. But again, she swooped down and tied, then untied, her laces.

According to the ribbons displayed along the wall, Pancho Villa won the California State Salsa Awards in 1999, 2000, 2001, 2002,

2003, 2004, 2005, 2006, 2007, 2009, 2010, 2011, 2012, and 2013. What went wrong with the salsa in 2008?

This woman is still messing with her shoe. I take a step closer and begin to crowd her. She's heavyset and wearing a long black coat and sweatpants. A logo-less baseball hat is pulled so low on her face I can't see her eyes. Sometimes she doesn't retie the shoe; sometimes she squeezes it as if she's in a shoe store and wants to make sure it fits right. I'm starving. Now I just want to strangle her. I take another step closer, and I'm sure at this point she can feel my breath on her neck. At last, she grabs her neat sack of leftovers and stands up. Pancho Villa doesn't have chairs, only these oddly comfortable leather stools. It's kind of like your ass is cradled in a little basket. I plunk down and assert my manifest destiny. I watch the woman walk the gauntlet between the packed tables toward the front of the taqueria, where the security guard opens the door for people coming and going. Only then does she look back at who took her seat, and only then do I see her eyes.

Let's pause a moment and take it all a little more slowly. I'm a guy who's hungry. I'm at the Pancho Villa. The place is crawling with depressed Giants fans. I'm alone. I just want to eat my burrito. I've got a new book, a memoir by Elias Canetti called *The Tongue Set Free.* Although in this atmosphere, I might as well be reading *Crowds and Power.* That's a bookish joke. Anyway, I picked up *The Tongue Set Free* at the Salvation Army on Valencia and Cesar Chavez for a buck-fifty. Normally, used hardcovers are three dollars, but all books are half off on red-tag Tuesdays. I want to read a section that I'm holding in place with my finger. It's called

"Father's Death: The Final Version." I scout a table against the wall. Looks like a woman is through eating. I like to eat against a wall, and I like to read in public. I think it's about anonymity. You read a book in public and it's like you don't exist. I'm nobody, just another guy in a flannel shirt with a book, which is what I am. (Too old to be a hipster, my facial hair is not planned out.) I'm impatient, not curious about what this shoe-tier's problem is, though it's obvious that there is something wrong, some psychic trouble in addition to whatever is the matter with her shoe. But this is not my concern. She's holding my table hostage. And so I close in on her, and she finally surrenders and stands and walks toward the door, and there's this moment, as I said, when she looks back at me.

Elias Canetti was seven when his father collapsed to the carpet during breakfast. He'd been reading the newspaper. Montenegro had just declared war on Turkey. His mother screamed, "Jacques! Jacques! Jacques!" and grabbed her head and tore at her hair. Immediately, Elias was sent across the street to the neighbors', where he began to speak with an older boy as if nothing had just happened. This older boy challenges Elias to climb a tree. Elias obliges. He's a pretty good tree climber. Something in the older boy's voice suggests he isn't. A little while later his mother runs across the street and shouts: "Your father's dead and here you are climbing trees!"

My own father's death lacked any such drama. He died at home in the room my brother and I, though we haven't lived in that house, much less slept in it, for more than thirty years, still call the "play-room." At a certain point in the early 1980s the playroom became my brother's room, which was a great honor, but even after that we still called it the playroom.

We never really knew each other, my father and I. It seems dishonorable, corrupt even, to be dragging myself around my adopted city as if I'm in mourning. But there you have it. He's been gone a year. I'm still trying to wander off my father's death. I used to justify my never answering the phone when he called by reminding myself that when I was a kid he used to call my mother that cunt. After my mother, brother, and I moved out of our house, the house my father died in, to the other side of town, my father would call and scream into the phone, and my brother, instead of hanging up on him (because if he did, he'd just call again), would shove the receiver into the utility drawer. Then we'd listen to him shouting cunt in the drawer amid the Bic pens, screwdrivers, Scotch tape, and loose change. I should let this go. There are other things to remember. What about how he used to arrive in a three-piece suit, topcoat, and furry hat to watch me play junior-high football? He looked like a German burgermeister. I played cornerback for the Little Giants. *Orner on the corner*, Coach Arreazola would say into his bullhorn. *Wake up, Orner on the corner! What do you think this is—naptime?* But my father was proud of me in my uniform and shoulder pads. And he didn't give a shit how he looked. Nor did he seem to notice, or care, when I ran *away* from the guy carrying the ball rather than toward him for a tackle.

He died in the playroom in a rented hospital bed it had taken four men to carry up the stairs. In the months before he died, he'd begun to hallucinate. At one point, he insisted there was a bear in the room. Black or brown? I asked. Brown, he said. Brown, I said, watch out, the brown ones are more dangerous. *Are you laughing at me? Can't you see this bear in here?*

* * *

Two months after he died there was an estate sale. A horde walked away with his stuff. One little man about my father's size stuffed all his Huntsman suits in a garbage bag and wrote a check for fifty dollars.

Last night, I sat in Pancho Villa on a comfortable stool. There, in all that light, I sat. Pancho Villa himself rides on a horse on top of the drinks cooler. On the back wall, near the bathrooms, he heigh-ho's across Chihuahua. At first, when the woman turned to look back, I thought she must have forgotten something. She wasn't looking at me, she was looking at the table she'd just left behind. I couldn't begin to describe to you what I saw in her eyes. She wasn't asking for help. She'd long ago stopped looking to other people, strangers or otherwise, for anything at all. It was only the table she wanted. She didn't want to go back out there on the street. Not yet. Pancho Villa closes at eleven. A few hours in the light would have made some difference. Buzzing, imprisoning light. But this, too, can be a haven.

Sources and Notes on the Notes

1. Sometimes I Believe We Are Being Tested

"Chekhov's Way of Dying": There are, of course, a great many translations of Chekhov's stories. Constance Garnett is often credited with bringing Chekhov to a large English-language audience, but has also been excoriated for being too stuffy. But here's the thing: Chekhov can pretty much survive anything, including a mediocre translation. In 1925, Virginia Woolf, reviewing a performance of *The Cherry Orchard*, said the interpretation of the play was off, the acting unnatural, the staging ridiculous—and still she left the theater shaken. "I do not know how better to describe the sensation at the end of *The Cherry Orchard* than by saying it sends one into the street feeling like a piano played upon at last, not in the middle but all over the keyboard and with the lid left open so the sound goes on." He reaches us from the Russian in spite of all the obstacles. The edition I've returned to over the years, and quoted here, is *Peasants and Other Stories* (New York: NYRB Classics, 1999), edited by Edmund Wilson and translated by Constance Garnett with revisions by Wilson. The book includes, in chronological order, Chekhov's last stories. More difficult to find is Chekhov's report on Sakhalin, but it is available: *Sakhalin Island* (London: Alma Classics, 2013), translated by Brian Reeve.

"A Bachelor Uncle" originally appeared in *The New York Times* under the title "A Relative Loss." The article about Nathan's Famous appeared in the *Shoreline*, Highland Park High School, sometime in the '80s.

"Winter in September": *The Stories of Breece D'J Pancake* (New York: Little, Brown, 1983), with an introduction by James Alan McPherson and an afterword by John Casey. Back Bay reprint edition published in 2002, with an additional essay on Pancake by Andre Dubus III.

"Wideman's Welcome": *All Stories Are True* (New York: Vintage Contemporaries, 1993). I like this edition because it is portable, but *All Stories Are True* is a condensed version of the hardcover edition of *The Stories of John Edgar Wideman* (New York: Pantheon, 1992), an essential collection of Wideman's work, which includes linked stories as well as stories like "Welcome" that stand alone.

"The Lonely Voice": Frank O'Connor's *The Lonely Voice: A Study of the Short Story* has appeared (and gone out of print) multiple times. The edition I use is *The Lonely Voice* (New York: Harper, 1985), with an introduction by Russell Banks. The book is currently published by Melville House. The latest edition came out in 2011. The translation of Gogol's "The Overcoat" I quoted is from *The Collected Tales of Nikolai Gogol* (New York: Vintage, 1999), translated by Richard Pevear and Larissa Volokhonsky.

"Stray Thoughts on Kafka": Diary entries are from *The Diaries of Franz Kafka* (London: Penguin, 1988). The Milena letter is from *Letters to Milena* (New York: Vintage Classics, 1982). Of the many translations of Kafka's stories, I prefer *Franz Kafka Stories, 1904–1924,* translated by J. A. Underwood, with a brief and priceless introduction by Jorge Luis Borges (London: Little, Brown, 1983). The story about Kafka's alleged son is from W. H. Auden, *The Dyer's Hand* (New York: Random House, 1962). I'd also commend to anyone with an interest in Kafka: *Conversations with Kafka* by Gustav Janouch (New York: New Directions, 2012), with an introduction by Francine Prose, a bizarre and delightful book that may or may not be an accurate factual account of the conversations the author, a young poet, had with Kafka during long walks across Prague. But as Prose nails it in the introduction, "Re-reading Janouch, I thought: If Kafka didn't say all these things, he said some of them and should have said the rest." Among the things Kafka said, or should have said, is this:

> Detective stories are always concerned with the solution of mysteries which are hidden behind extraordinary occurrences. But in real life it's absolutely the opposite. The mystery isn't hidden in the background. On the contrary! It stares one in the face. It's what is obvious. So we do not see it. Everyday life is the greatest detective story ever written.

"Eudora Welty, Badass": "No Place for You, My Love," and "The Burning" appear in the collection *The Bride of the Innisfallen* (New York: Harcourt Brace, 1955), as well as in *The Collected Stories of Eudora Welty* (New York: Harcourt Brace, 1982). The early e-mail program Eudora was named after Welty, in honor of her story "Why I Live at the P.O."

"Walser on Mission Street": *Selected Stories of Robert Walser* (New York: New York Review of Books, 2002), introduction by Susan Sontag and postscript by Christopher Middleton. We're in the midst of a Walser renaissance. A new edition of his work seems to come out every year of late. In edition to the *Selected Stories*, I highly recommend *Microscripts* (New York: New Directions, 2010), translated by Susan Bernofsky with an afterword by Walter Benjamin, an edition of very short pieces, complete with breathtaking images of Walser's tiny writing. The W. G. Sebald quote is from "Le Promeneur Solitaire: On Robert Walser," from the posthumous essay collection *A Place in the Country* (New York: Random House,

2013), translated by Jo Catling. "The Marquise of O," in all its rollicking grandeur, can be found in *The Marquise of O and Other Stories* (London: Penguin Classics, 1978), translated by David Luke and Nigel Reeves.

"On the Beauty of Not Writing": I'm partial to the translation of "Luvina" in Rulfo's *The Burning Plain and Other Stories* (Austin: University of Texas Press, 1967), translated by George D. Schade, with eerie illustrations by Kermit Oliver. Recently the collection has been reissued as *The Plain in Flames* (Austin: University of Texas Press, 2012), translated by Ilan Stavans with Harold Augenbraum. My partiality may well come from having encountered the Schade version first. Sometimes it is difficult to fall in love with a new translation after spending so much time with an older one. Both, in different ways, capture the soulful starkness of Rulfo's language. I'd split the difference and have both copies on the shelf. The Chekhov quote is from one of his earliest longer stories, "The Steppe" (1888). It's about a boy who sits in the back of a cart and listens to the men talk and talk and talk . . .

2. Let Me Cook You an Egg

"Upper Moose Lake, 1990": *To the Lighthouse* (New York: Harcourt, 1989), with an introduction by Eudora Welty. Welty writes that no matter how ethereal the novel gets, Woolf always tethers the story to the earth with "an iron clamp." Originally appeared in *Salon*.

"My Father's Gloves": Originally appeared in *The New York Times*.

"Unforgivable": William Maxwell's "With Reference to an Incident at a Bridge" may be found in the Maxwell collection *Billie Dyer and Other Stories* (New York: Plume, 1993), as well as in *All the Days and*

Nights: The Collected Stories of William Maxwell (New York: Vintage, 1995) and *William Maxwell's Later Stories and Novels* (New York: Modern Library, 2008). See also Maxwell's hymn to reading in "Nearing Ninety," published in *The New York Times* in 1997, where, in one of his final gifts, he writes the following:

> Before I am ready to call it quits I would like to reread every book I have ever deeply enjoyed, beginning with Jane Austen and going through shelf after shelf of the bookcases, until I arrive at the "Autobiographies" of William Butler Yeats. As it is, I read a great deal of the time. I am harder to please, though. I see flaws in masterpieces. Conrad indulging in rhetoric when he would do better to get on with it. I would read all day long and well into the night if there were no other claims on my time.

"While Reading Imre Kertész": The short novel *Kaddish for a Child Not Born* is available in at least two translations: by Christopher C. Wilson and Katharina M. Wilson (Evanston: Northwestern, 1977), and by Tim Wilkinson under the title *Kaddish for an Unborn Child* (New York: Random House, 2004). Northwestern's translation came out first (before Kertész won the Nobel Prize; hand it to small presses for often spotting great work before the monoliths), but I can't say I'm partial to it since I have yet to read the new version. I will say, though the book may have once put me to sleep, I will never forget it. Originally appeared in *Guernica*.

"Under All This Noise": The Herbert Morris poem "History, Weather, Loss, the Children, Georgia" may be found in his final collection, *What Was Lost* (Berkeley: Counterpoint, 2000). The film *Say Anything* (1989) was written and directed by Cameron Crowe. Hail Lloyd Dobler. See also: Eudora Welty, *The Eye of the Story:*

Essays and Reviews (New York: Vintage, 1990). Originally appeared in *The Millions.*

"Hit and Run": William Trevor's "The Dressmaker's Child" appears in *Cheating at Canasta* (New York: Viking, 2007). A brief word on Trevor: I wonder sometimes if we don't take him for granted, as if somewhere in the back of our minds, we loyal readers of his work believe the man might be immortal. Trevor has been writing so well for so long. All the stories ("The Piano Tuner's Wives," "Lovers of Their Time," "The News from Ireland"). All the novels (*Fools of Fortune, The Story of Lucy Gault, Felicia's Journey*). In the margin of the title page of my mammoth *Collected Stories* (which is no longer the collected stories, as he's written at least four collections since), I wrote a note to myself: "Think about the way he takes responsibility for strangers." This says it better than what I managed to say about "The Dressmaker's Child."

"Carter on Borden": Angela Carter died too young at fifty-one. Readers were robbed. She turned fairy tales back into nightmares, where they belong. "The Fall River Axe Murders" may be found in *Saints and Strangers* (New York: Viking, 1986), as well as in Carter's *Burning Your Boats: The Collected Stories* (London: Penguin, 1997), with an introduction by Salman Rushdie.

"Shameless Impostors": "My Son the Murderer" may be found in *Rembrandt's Hat* (1973) and *The Complete Stories* (New York: FSG Classics, 1998). The quote from *The Brothers Karamazov* is from the Pevear and Volokhonsky translation (New York: Farrar, Straus and Giroux, 2002).

"The Infinite Passion of Gina Berriault": "Around the Dear Ruin" first appeared in book form in *The Mistress and Other Stories* (New

York: Dutton, 1965), and seventeen years later in *The Infinite Passion of Expectation* (San Francisco: North Point, 1982), and again in *Women in Their Beds: New and Selected Stories* (Berkeley: Counterpoint, 1997). In a rare interview Berriault granted in the 1980s, she was asked a similar question to the one Juan Rulfo was so often asked: Why the long silence? Berriault answered, "That's a question that should never be asked. It opens a wound. What can a writer say about gaps and silence?" *The Tea Ceremony: Uncollected Writings of Gina Berriault* (Washington, D.C.: Shoemaker and Hoard, 2003), introduction by Leonard Gardner, author of *Fat City*. Her publisher has reissued *Three Short Novels* (Berkeley: Counterpoint, 2014), which includes *The Lights of the Earth*, which, to my mind, is among the most wrenching novels ever written about San Francisco and points north, including Bolinas.

"Since the Beginning of Time": "The Tramp Steamer's Last Port of Call" may be found in *The Adventures and Misadventures of Maqroll* (New York: NYRB Classics, 2002), translated by Edith Grossman. See also an interview with Mutis by Francisco Goldman in *Bomb* magazine, 2001.

> **Goldman:** *Is there anything in this world as beautiful as a tramp steamer?*
>
> **Mutis:** *(laughter)* No, there isn't . . . well, not anymore. You know, when I see one, and I see them often when I travel, it brings tears to my eyes.

Originally appeared in *ZYZZYVA*.

"Surviving the Lives We Have": Dubus's *Voices from the Moon* was originally published as a short novel (Boston: Godine, 1984) and subsequently included in *Selected Stories* (New York: Vintage, 1995).

"Every Grief-Soaked Word": Zora Neale Hurston's *Their Eyes Were Watching God* (New York: Harper, 2006). I remain loyal to the first (borrowed/stolen) edition of Isaac Babel that I read, *The Collected Stories* (New York: Meridian Books, 1960), introduction by Lionel Trilling. I think it remains the best, although *Collected Stories*, translated by David McDuff (London: Penguin, 1996), is without a doubt more accurate, since it is based, unlike Morrison's, on a later, uncensored edition of Babel's collected works in Russian. I keep both editions close. In the piece, I also referred to a rare first edition of *The Red Cavalry* in English, translated by Nadia Helstein (New York: Knopf, 1929), and to the very latest translation of *Red Cavalry*, by Boris Dralyuk (London: Pushkin Press, 2014), which I welcome, as it brings back some of the antic energy captured by the earlier Morrison version. Babel's long-awaited *The Complete Stories of Isaac Babel* (New York: Norton, 2005), translated by Peter Constantine, with essays by Natalie Babel and Cynthia Ozick, is an important and necessary book because it collects all of Babel's work in one place and includes nonfiction, plays, filmscripts, and novel fragments. Yet *The Complete Stories* was panned by many Babelians, and with good reason, because the prose, in English, is rhythmically off. My hunch is that the stories were translated with too much confidence. They often feel, I don't know how else to say it, *translated*. But as Roberto Bolaño once said, echoing Virginia Woolf's response to Chekhov: How do you recognize if a piece of literature is a work of art?

> Easy. Let it be translated. Let its translator be far from brilliant. Rip pages from it at random. Leave it lying in an attic. If after all this a kid comes along and reads it, and after reading makes it his own, and is faithful to it (or unfaithful, whichever) and reinterprets it and accompanies it on its voyage to the edge, and both are enriched and the kid adds

an ounce of value to its original value, then we have something before us ...

—*Between Parentheses*

(New York: New Directions, 2011),

translated by Natasha Wimmer

That's the power of Babel, even the Constantine version. For all its
lack of cadence, the stories still burst forth on the page. I imagine
a translation, any translation, of *Their Eyes Were Watching God*
might have the same sort of impact on a reader stumbling across
the book in a local branch library in Bucharest. The letter from
Babel is quoted from *The Lonely Years* (New York: FSG, 1964). The
translation of Radovan Karadžić's poetry comes from Jay Surdukowski's fascinating article on the militaristic poetry of talentless
poets: "Is Poetry a War Crime? Reckoning for Radovan Karadžić"
(*Michigan Journal of International Law*, Vol. 26, 2005), thanklessly
translated by Surdukowski. The anecdote about Stalin calling Ilya
Ehrenburg appeared in "Isaac Babel and His Daughter" by James
Salter in *The Paris Review*, No. 137 (1995).

"A Black Boy, a White Boy": The work of Wright Morris, after being
issued initially by major publishers, has been kept in print over the
years by a number of small presses, including Black Sparrow, David
R. Godine, and the University of Nebraska Press. "A Fight Between
a White Boy and a Black Boy in the Dusk of a Fall Afternoon in
Omaha, Nebraska" may be found in *Collected Stories (1948–1986)*
(Boston: Godine, 1989). See also a novel I could not live without:
Plains Song: For Female Voices (Lincoln: University of Nebraska,
2000), with a generous introduction by Charles Baxter.

"A Small Note from Haiti": *Street of Lost Footsteps* (Lincoln: University of Nebraska, 2003), translated by Linda Coverdale. See also

Children of Heroes (Lincoln: University of Nebraska Press, 2008). To date, Lyonel Trouillot's many other novels remain untranslated from the French. The interview with Trouillot is excerpted from *Lavil: Life, Love, and Death in Port-au-Prince*, forthcoming from Voice of Witness/McSweeney's and Verso, edited by Peter Orner and Evan Lyon.

3. And Here You Are Climbing Trees

"Mad Passionate True Love": The play *Largo Desolato* may be found in Havel's *Selected Plays: 1963–1983* (New York: Grove, 1987), translated by Tom Stoppard. *Letters to Olga* (New York: Knopf, 1988), translated by Paul Wilson. See also a recent biography of Havel called *Havel: A Life* by Michael Žantovský (New York: Grove, 2014).

"Frederick the Great" appeared in a German translation in *Die Literarische Welt* (Berlin). I've never been able to discover the name of the relative.

"An American Writer: Victor Martinez": Another far too early loss. Martinez died in San Francisco at the age of fifty-six on February 18, 2011. We used to go to SF MOMA together. Victor would stare at a painting for a while and say, if he liked it, "This one's honest." The complete poem "Don't Forget" may be found in *Caring for a House* (San Jose: Chusma House, 1992). Martinez's now classic novel about growing up in Fresno, *Parrot in the Oven*, remains in print, as I hope it will forever (New York: Harper Collins, 2004).

"Cheever in Albania": *The World of Apples* (New York: Knopf, 1973). "The World of Apples" was reprinted in the big red *The Stories of John Cheever* (New York: Vintage, 2000).

"All Lives Are Interesting": Mavis Gallant's essay "Paul Léautaud, 1872–1956" may be found in *Paris Notebooks* (New York: Random House, 1988), and "In Plain Sight" in *Collected Stories* (New York: Random House, 1996), as well as in *Paris Stories* (New York: NYRB Classics, 2002). Portions of this essay appeared in *The Rumpus*, as well as in *The Atlantic's* "By Heart" column edited by Joe Fassler.

"Sisters and Brothers": Saul Bellow's "The Old System" may be found in *Mosby's Memoirs* (New York: Viking, 1996) and in *Collected Stories* (New York: Penguin, 2001), edited by Janis Bellow, with an introduction by James Wood

"Parting": Heinrich Böll's "Parting" may be found in *Collected Stories* (Evanston: Northwestern University Press, 1995), translated by Leila Vennewitz.

"What Feels Like the World": Richard Bausch's story "What Feels Like the World" may be found in *Spirits and Other Stories* (New York: Simon and Schuster, 1987), as well as in *The Stories of Richard Bausch* (New York: Harper, 2004). Tobias Wolff's "Bullet in the Brain" may be found in *The Night in Question* (New York: Vintage, 1997).

"Virgie Walking Away": "The Wanderers" is the final story in *The Golden Apples* (New York: Harcourt, Brace and Company, 1949). The book as a whole reappears in Welty's *Collected Stories* (New York: Harcourt Brace, 1982). But what is *The Golden Apples*? A collection of stories or a novel? I'd say *The Golden Apples* is a radically unconventional novel held together by common characters moving in entirely different directions. Read "The Wanderers" by itself, it is a moving story; read it in the context of the entire book, and the impact is overwhelming.

"Cincinnati, 2001": A. S. Byatt's *The Matisse Stories* (New York: Vintage, 1996) is a kind of book-length response to Matisse through fiction. In a story called "The Chinese Lobster," an old painter tells the story of how as a young man on the make he once visited Matisse.

> "The rooms in that apartment were shrouded in darkness. The shutters were closed, the curtains were drawn. I was terribly shocked—I thought he *lived in the light*, you know, that was the idea I had of him. I blurted it out, the shock, I said, 'Oh, how can you bear to shut out the light?' And he said, quite mildly, quite courteously, that there had been some question of him going blind. And then he added, 'and anyway, you know, black is the color of light.'"

But with this particular book, all I need is to see the light blue cover and it sends me back to another time. Originally appeared in *No Tokens*.

"Salter": James Salter, *Dusk* (New York: Modern Library, 2011), *Light Years* (New York: Vintage, 1994), and *All That Is* (New York: Vintage, 2014). It is said that Salter changed his name in order to pass. This may be true. But I also wonder if he changed it less to deny a Jewish identity than because of a desire not to be handcuffed by it. Everybody deserves a shot at not being themselves. If not for a lifetime, at least once in a while.

"Early Morning Thoughts on Ahab": The only way to read *Moby-Dick* is to read it alongside the illustrations by Rockwell Kent (New York: Modern Library, 1992). The Yoel Hoffmann quote is from Hoffmann's *Moods* (New York: New Directions, 2015). Hoffmann is often referred to, in marketing material, as Israel's "leading experimental novelist." The tag does this writer's work a disservice by placing it in an imaginary category, as if all experimental novels were somehow written in the same vein, which seems contrary to the spirit of experimentation. Hoffmann's work is uniquely and weirdly intimate and strange, I'll grant this. But all great work is experimental. *Moby-Dick* remains among America's most innovative, unconventional—and, of course, experimental—novels.

"All Fathers Are Fictional": *Love and Shame and Love* (New York: Little, Brown, 2011). Originally appeared in *Buzzfeed*.

"Ronald A. Orner": The Ronald Orner obituary appeared in *The Highland Park News*, Highland Park, Illinois.

"Letter from New Melleray, Iowa": François Charles Mauriac, *Life of Jesus* (London: Hodder & Stoughton, 1937). Mauriac once said, "What I fear is not being forgotten after my death, but, rather, not being enough forgotten." Originally appeared in *McSweeney's*.

"A Palm-of-the-Hand Story": *Snow Country* (New York: Vintage, 1984), translated by Edward G. Seidensticker, and *Palm-of-the-Hand Stories* (New York: North Point, 1988), translated by Lane Dunlop and J. Martin Holman. There is some dispute over whether Kawabata committed suicide. There are some who have suggested that the gas was left on by accident. What is certain is that he was preoccupied by suicide throughout his life, and quoted, in his Nobel address, a line from the suicide note of one of the pioneers of the modern Japanese short story, Ryūnosuke Akutagawa:

> But nature is for me more than it has ever been before. I have no doubt that you will laugh at the contradiction, for here I love nature even when I am contemplating suicide. But

nature is beautiful because it comes to my eyes in their last extremity.

"Night Train to Split": Bohumil Hrabal, *Too Loud a Solitude* (New York: Harcourt, 1990), translated by Michael Henry Heim. Hrabal, as well, may or may not have committed suicide. At the age of eighty-eight, he fell, or jumped, out of a fifth-story hospital room window. Some say he was only trying to feed the pigeons, but I wonder if he may have wanted to do both, end his life and feed the pigeons. See also Hrabal's *Pirouettes on a Postage Stamp: An Interview Novel with Questions Asked and Answers Recorded by László Szigeti* (Prague: Charles University Press, 2008), translated by David Short. In it he says, "You know, Mr. Szigeti, without a crack in the brain I can't live."

"Father's Death: The Final Version": Elias Canetti, *The Tongue Set Free* (London: Granta Books, 2011), translated by Joachim Neugroschel. Considered one of the most reclusive writers of the twentieth century, Canetti died in 1994 at the age of eighty-nine. He is buried next to James Joyce in Zurich. I imagine this has made him less reclusive.

Unless otherwise stated, most of these notes appeared, in very different form, as part of an irregular column called "The Lonely Voice" on Rumpus.net between 2008 and 2015.

Acknowledgments

I've always been moved by Salinger's dedication in *Raise High the Roof Beam, Carpenters* and *Seymour: An Introduction*: "If there is an amateur reader still left in the world—or anybody who just reads and runs—I ask him or her, with untellable affection and gratitude, to split the dedication of this book four ways . . ." In this spirit, I'd like to mention here a number of people without whom this book, or any of my previous ones, would not exist. Since I was a kid, I've watched my brother Eric Orner draw. All those hours and hours watching him, copying him, and I didn't, as my daughter will attest, absorb a microscopic speck of his talent. But if I've come to believe that stories are as essential as air, and I do, it is because of my brother, who tells them better than anybody—the very brother who stayed up late, and got up early, to finish the beautiful illustrations of the book covers. These are books that I've loved and I also have great affection for the objects themselves. So I asked my brother to repaint them in homage to the original artists. One could not ask for a more supportive champion than Ellen Levine, an agent who, above all, loves literature. And Pat Strachan, an editor who has not only put up with me for seventeen years and counting but is also brilliant, generous, and patient. Thanks to Dantia MacDonald, whose bravery cannot be measured. I consider myself beyond lucky to have had the following teachers: David Krause, Tish O'Dowd, Charles Baxter, Marilynne Robinson, and James Alan McPherson (rest peacefully, Jim). If there's a single line in this book that resonates, it's because they showed the way—and continue to show the way. What clunks is all on me. Thanks to Stephen Elliot, Isaac Fitzgerald, Zoë Ruiz, and Marisa Siegal of *The Rumpus* for the gift of absolute freedom in allowing the Lonely Voice to speak, as well as to Rhoda and Dan Pierce, Alex Gordon, David Krause (again), Katie Kane, Dave Eggers, Nick Regiacorte, Chris Abani, Melissa Kirsch, Eddy Loiseau, Matt Goshko, and Rob Preskill. Thanks to John McGhee and Lynn Warshow for such careful attention. Thanks also to the Passa Porta International House of Literature in Brussels for the grant of time and space. Finally, boundless thanks to Katie Crouch, unsung hero of these pages and so much else, and, of course, to Phoebe Kaplan Crouch Orner. (Bobo, we apologize for the endless name, we were only trying to cover all our bases.) And to my late father. There's a moment in Gina Berriault's "The Light at Birth" when an old woman on the rim of death circles back to the moment she was born. "Visions of light and of luminous strangers in that light—that was what the dying saw," Berriault writes. "They were the first of many strangers in your life, the ones there when you come out of the dark womb into the amazing light of earth, and never to be seen again in just that way until your last hours." Dad, I hope there was light, I really do.

Author and Title Index

Page numbers beginning with 295 refer to endnotes.

About the Author

Peter Orner is the author of two collections of stories, *Last Car Over the Sagamore Bridge* and *Esther Stories*, and two novels, *Love and Shame and Love* and *The Second Coming of Mavala Shikongo*. His stories and essays have appeared in many periodicals, including *The Atlantic, The New York Times, Granta, McSweeney's,* and *The Paris Review*, as well as in *The Best American Short Stories*. He has received the Rome Prize from the American Academy of Arts and Letters and the Bard Fiction Prize, and has been a finalist for the Hemingway Foundation/PEN Award, the New York Public Library Young Lions Fiction Award, and the *Los Angeles Times* Book Prize. Orner has received Guggenheim and Lannan Foundation Fellowships, and two Pushcart Prizes. He teaches in the graduate MFA program at San Francisco State University, lives in Bolinas, California, and is a member of the Bolinas Volunteer Fire Department.

About the Illustrator

Eric Orner is a cartoonist whose comics and graphic stories have appeared in many newspapers, magazines, and anthologies, including *Best American Comics, The Boston Globe, The Washington Post, The New Republic, McSweeney's,* and the *San Francisco Chronicle*. His long-running indy comic strip *The Mostly Unfabulous Social Life of Ethan Green* has been anthologized in five books, most recently, *The Completely Unfabulous Social Life of Ethan Green*, and was adapted as a feature film in 2005. By day, Eric is an attorney who worked for ten years on the staff of Congressman Barney Frank.